Praise for John Bil and *Ship to Shore*

"John unlocked stories of the water and always surprised us with his constant delicious treasures. Spending a night with his wild workmanship made you feel as if you'd found yourself inside the belly of a whale. With this book, we are incredibly lucky to be given the gift of his in-depth knowledge of the industry, along with his super power of making the simplest thing taste perfect. No tricks, all heart — like the way the sea penetrates your skin just by walking beside it — he had a way of salting the atmosphere. Let's dive in. Thank you, John." — Amy Millan, musician (Broken Social Scene, Stars)

"I've been waiting for a book like this for years and can't think of a better, more trustworthy author to write it. John Bil's knowledge about all things seafood was matched only by his love for the subject. This book is a fitting testament to him and an important addition to every food lover's collection." — Chris Johns, food writer and co-author of *True North: Canadian Cooking from Coast to Coast*

"Learning from John is a privilege, and this book will inspire you. Happy reading." — Martin Picard, chef/owner, Au Pied de Cochon

"If you eat a great oyster in North America, one that's sourced well and served right, so it's plump and intact and brimming with its own liquor, so it tastes as fresh and distinct as the bay where it grew, there's a good chance John Bil had a hand in that experience. As a travelling ambassador for P.E.I. oysters, and later as an unconventional Mr. Fix-It to top chefs and restaurateurs, he taught a generation of eaters not only how to serve and experience the world's best shellfish and seafood, but how to appreciate life." — Chris Nuttall-Smith, food writer

"If you care about seafood, Canada, or just being a good person, you should read this book. If you're an asshole, move along." — Matty Matheson, chef, TV personality, and author of *Matty Matheson: A Cookbook*

"John once said to me, 'Have you ever seen a fifteen-pound lobster? It's kind of terrifying. They could make a movie out of it. *Claws*.' He had an unparalleled depth of knowledge when it came to Canadian seafood." — Derek Dammann, chef/owner, Maison Publique and McKiernan, and co-author of *True North: Canadian Cooking from Coast to Coast*

"The philosophy and practices at M. Wells are forever shaped by our friendship with John Bil. He hoisted us into his boat, sharing with us countless adventures and wisdom along the way. In life John was a finisher; quite simply, he got things done — wonderful, thoughtful, miraculous things, as this book so beautifully attests." — Hugue Dufour and Sarah Obraitis, M. Wells Steakhouse

SHIP TO SHORE

STRAIGHT TALK FROM THE SEAFOOD COUNTER

JOHN BIL

FOREWORD BY FRÉDÉRIC MORIN

PHOTOGRAPHY BY RICK O'BRIEN

AMBROSIA

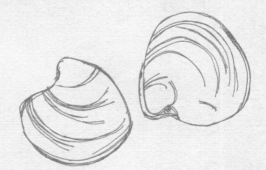

Published in Canada in 2018 and the USA in 2018
by House of Anansi Press Inc.
www.houseofanansi.com

Library and Archives Canada Cataloguing in
Publication

Bil, John, author
    Ship to shore: straight talk from the seafood
counter / John Bil.

Issued in print and electronic formats.
ISBN 978-1-4870-0413-2 (hardcover).—ISBN
978-1-4870-0414-9 (EPUB).—ISBN 978-1-4870-
0415-6 (Kindle)

1. Cooking (Seafood). 2. Seafood. 3. Cookbooks.
I. Title.

TX747.B54 2018   641.6'92   C2018-900658-7
C2018-900659-5

Library of Congress Control Number: 2018931742

Book design: Greg Tabor

Front cover and interior photographs: Rick O'Brien,
with the exception of images listed here: pages x
and 5 courtesy of Sheila Flaherty; pages xiv and
112 courtesy of Johnny C.Y. Lam; pages 5, 83
(StockFood/Rapado, Miriam), 29 (iStockPhoto
/ chameleonseye), 106 (StockFood/Spairani,
Alessandra), 116 (iStockPhoto/nastenkin), 122
(StockFood/Tang-Evans, Ming), 142 (Design Pics
Inc/Alamy Stock Photo), 157 (StockFood/Leh-
mann, Joerg), 164 (StockFood / Shippen, Mick),
173 (The Picture Pantry/Alamy Stock Photo),
174 (Denis Karpenkov/Alamy Stock Photo), 178
(StockFood/New, Myles), 181 (age fotostock/
Alamy Stock Photo), 189 (StockFood/Atelier
Mai 98), 230 (StockFood/Kirchherr, Jo), 233
(Bon Appetit/Alamy Stock Photo), 242 (Nopadol
Uengbunchoo/Alamy Stock Photo), 244 (Picture
Pantry / Lisovskaya Natalia), and 257 (Massi-
mo Lama / Alamy Stock Photo); and page 260
courtesy of Sea to Table.

Illustrations: pages vi, 24, and 25 by John Petcoff,
page ix (iStockPhoto/ilbusca); pages 7, 103, 143,
233, and endpapers (iStockPhoto/Ruskpp)
Back cover photograph: David De Stefano

Canada Council   Conseil des Arts
for the Arts   du Canada

ONTARIO ARTS COUNCIL
CONSEIL DES ARTS DE L'ONTARIO
an Ontario government agency
un organisme du gouvernement de l'Ontario

We acknowledge for their financial support of our
publishing program the Canada Council for the
Arts, the Ontario Arts Council, and the Government of Canada.

Printed and bound in Canada

FSC
www.fsc.org

MIX
Paper from
responsible sources
FSC® C016245

This book is for you.

By asking the questions and pushing the boundaries,
we can all celebrate John Bil's work and his dedication
to the betterment of the industry. Read this book, feed people
around your table, and continue to cherish the wild
and wonderful world in the water.

From the bottom of our hearts, thank you.

-CONTENTS-

FOREWORD

Being that John was the first person I knew to own a phone with a qwerty keyboard, my friends and I became heavily reliant on his inquisitive and curious mind. John had the tools and the smarts to find us the best Italian food, the most decorated tulip breeder, and the right selection of quirky documentaries to watch after the *poulet au vin jaune* got the best of us. Unavoidably, the documentary we'd select would inspire us to make our own — one day, we'd say. The closest we got to it was a compendium of images and clichés, with a soundtrack à la *Chef's Table*, wherein the viewer stays on their toes until the final intrigue is solved, and all along, it turns out, you weren't watching a movie about Bordeaux or some counterfeit drummer — it was, after the screechy modem sounds, the Philip Glass loops of anxious minor keys, and the apocalyptic visuals of giant fans, a simple documentary about two guys. Two refrigeration technicians looking for gas for an old compressor.

That was John. In many ways never content with just watching a doc, he wanted to make one. Of course, that's also the story of two dudes sitting on a couch, having consumed too many morels and fruit spirits — but that was his essence, the distillate of his mind. He approached oysters, fish, sea creatures, and ocean disasters with the same competitive curiosity.

I met John on the phone, twenty years ago. I called the oyster plant where he worked, briefly expressed my love for the oysters he was shipping, and three days later received an order — no account-opening, no COD. Up until then, it was in vogue to top oysters artistically but nonsensically with jellies and balls of various exotic fruit. John sourced and shuttled such divine specimens that I felt shame for ever having squeezed wasabi

John Bil with Frédéric Morin and David McMillan of Joe Beef.

mayo on a mangled oyster! Over the years that followed, our tradition was a succession of Sunday dinners with friends — later mostly with Allison and the kids, and Sheila — and always, as the ritual demands, followed by clear fruit spirits and wacky documentaries!

The book you are holding in your hands, he wrote it all — checked out of the hospital to pick up the sturgeon and lay it out on the floor at home, propping its head up so that it looked pretty! I had not read the book before, and I had no doubts that John would write something great. Then he asked me to write a foreword and all that came to mind was sorry loads of power metaphors and shamefully boring oyster puns.

This book, as most of John's work, leaves aside the anecdotal science and the clichés. A solid, logic-based look at the often-discussed issue of sustainability is what we have here. John and I shared an almost nihilist outlook on food at times, avoiding hopping on bandwagon trends, favouring instead the sempiternal devil's advocate view. But the critical lens he viewed food through did not feel as such once you were running an oyster bar, or found yourself on either side of one! His knowledge, wit, and love made John Bil an excellent host, guest, and dining companion. A man willing to loudly tout and express his love of sweet wines and lamprey eel must be praised!

John was my best friend. I've done my best to provide a few words that can live up to him, and I'm glad he wrote this book. Every once in a while, when I miss being schooled and scolded about oysters, I'll pick it up, show my kids and friends, and tell them I knew the man . . . then proceed to school them.

FRÉDÉRIC MORIN
MONTREAL
MAY 2018

INTRODUCTION

In the summer of 1992, my friend John Petcoff opened an outpost of Rodney's Oyster House, a popular Toronto seafood restaurant, in Cavendish, Prince Edward Island. I'd worked with John for a few years at the flagship Rodney's, so when he invited me out East to help with the new operation, I jumped at the opportunity. I was immediately captivated by the people, the landscape, and, of course, the food. But even more than this, I connected with the farming side of seafood. Observing the numerous communities, fishers, and affiliated businesses that depended upon fish as a resource, I saw another side of Canada. And I began to understand that the fisheries must be promoted and managed with care to ensure their survival. After that first summer, I returned to the Maritimes for a couple more seasons. Then, in 1995, I finally took the plunge and moved there full time, with a van, no plan, and very little money.

It isn't easy for an outsider to move to Prince Edward Island and get a job in the oyster business. The low wages, harsh working conditions, and isolation all take a toll, and can make you doubt your decision and yourself. Luckily, I'd made a few connections working at Rodney's and was offered a job at Carr's Lobster Pound, one of a handful of seafood buyers and growers who dealt primarily in lobsters, clams, and oysters. Since I knew exactly zero about growing or fishing oysters, the only job available to me was on the plant floor. It paid $7.50 an hour, and mostly involved scraping and sorting oysters in a cold, stark packing plant. There were no windows, and the water ran constantly at an ocean-ambient temperature (during winter it was often 0°C/32°F on the floor). I'd punch in at eight o'clock, work for two hours, have a coffee in the tiny break room (exactly fifteen minutes), lunch for thirty minutes in the same room, break again at three o'clock, and then clock out at six — six days a week.

I was taking home around $1,000 a month, but my truck payments and rent ate up almost 60 percent of that, leaving me with just $100 a week for everything else. It was a tough life compared to what I'd had going in Toronto, but no different from that of many folks out East. I was lonely and broke, and not always entirely sure what I'd gotten myself into. But Robert and Phyllis, the owners of Carr's, were great people who looked out for me and really tried to help me when they could. Gradually, they gave me more responsibility and things got a little easier. Though the hours and working conditions didn't improve, the pay did a little, as I became

John Petcoff working a vintage Alaska Ice Crusher.

more useful. Soon, I was out on the boats tonging oysters off the lease, and driving around the island, picking up oysters from various fishers and growers. I began to understand and appreciate how tricky oysters are to grow. I learned about the importance of bottom conditions, when not to transfer oysters, why they change flavour throughout the year, and that different rivers and bays yield different results. It was an amazing few years.

Eventually, I moved to a larger farm, where I began working in sales. I started talking by phone to customers all over North America, and soon I was hitting the road to meet with distributors and chefs, attend trade shows, and visit other farms to observe their operations. But after more than ten years in the P.E.I. oyster business, plus a few more working in the salmon industry in New Brunswick, I was ready for a change.

In August 2005, I received an email from a chef friend in Montreal who I'd become close to after years of selling him oysters. Fred Morin wrote to say that he was finally opening a restaurant with his partner, Dave McMillan, and asked if I would be willing to leave the Maritimes, move to Montreal, and give them a hand. The restaurant was Joe Beef.

Tucked away in a then-sleepy corner of Montreal, Joe Beef was a passion project from the beginning. The six of us who made up the original crew were in it together, come hell or high water, for friendship. I had given up a stable life in the Maritimes, I couldn't speak French, and my only friends in Montreal were the people in the restaurant. I was going to teach them everything I knew about seafood — how to source it and

John hosting a backyard clambake on P.E.I.

how to cook it — and they were going to teach me everything else. I had always been an enthusiastic home cook, and had hung out in restaurants here and there, but the immersive education I got from Fred and Dave was like nothing I'd ever experienced. I'll never describe myself as a chef because I will never know as much as Fred.

With Joe Beef a success, Fred and Dave decided to open a second spot, Liverpool House. While they threw their energy into the new place, I looked after Joe Beef. Everyone came out a winner. Over the next few years, I helped to open a place in New York City, and then returned to the Maritimes to open a restaurant of my own in P.E.I. called Ship to Shore. But always I returned to Montreal to work with my brothers Fred and Dave.

After a few years in the restaurant business,

I started a small seafood import company back home in Toronto. By 2012, the Toronto restaurant scene was exploding, and I felt I could supply some high-quality niche products. Business progressed well, and with my partner, Victoria Bazan, Honest Weight was born. Victoria and I knew each other from P.E.I., and we shared a vision of putting a fresh face on seafood, for both the retail and restaurant markets. From the beginning, the philosophy was to purchase thoughtfully, pay staff equitably, and be as transparent as possible with the products served and sold. The idea is for everyone to buy more fish! Honest Weight's goal is to be part of a new movement in fish-selling — a movement that values quality over economy, that understands the costs of ignoring the science around fish stock health, and that can find room for both carefully caught wild fish and ethically farmed fish and shellfish.

The business of fish is all about trust and confidence. We all know how to buy ground beef or chicken breasts. And, for the most part, we know what to do with them when we get them home. Fish — and shellfish, of course; to me, they are all fish — on the other hand, come from so many different places and take so many different forms. It's very common to see salmon from Canada, Norway, and Chile displayed side by side in the grocery store. But you would never see the same confusing origins in the chicken section. And variety! Lobster next to mussels and oysters, alongside whole sardines and five kinds of fillets. No wonder we generally leave it to restaurants to deal with our fish. Life is complicated enough, so let's just make burgers tonight, okay?

I feel my years of experience "on the water" have helped Honest Weight build trust with the people who come into the shop. I know how confusing fish can be, but I want customers to leave with something. I'm motivated, and I'm more than happy to spend twenty minutes teaching someone how to open an oyster just to get them to buy six. To me, all the items in the fish case are as normal as a T-bone steak, and my goal is to make customers feel that way about them, too. It won't happen overnight, but if we can keep people coming back, we've got a shot.

WITH THIS BOOK, I want to pull back the curtain on the business of fish, to help you understand why fish costs what it does, and to make your life easier and less stressful when you're staring at the seemingly endless options at the fish counter. I've handled and cooked a lot of different fish over the years, so I'd also like to give you the confidence to try new fish, to discover how delicious they can be, or to do new things with the fish that you already know and love.

To make things simpler, I've separated the book into four sections: shellfish (clams, lobster, oysters), small fish (herring, mackerel, sardines), medium fish (cod, haddock, trout), all the way up to my larger favourites (halibut, swordfish, tuna). Within these pages, you'll find recipes for a variety of fish and shellfish, of course, but I've also attempted to convey which species may be in trouble and which are healthy. My goal is to demystify fish, to give you the confidence to branch out, to convince you to buy fish that you may not have considered, and maybe even to stop you from buying things that might be contributing to solvable problems. I want to get you excited about the vast amount of amazing fish that's out there.

I love the stuff, and I want you to as well.

JOHN BIL
TORONTO
DECEMBER 2017

SHELLFISH

So many different creatures get lumped into the category of "shellfish" that it can be a little overwhelming. In this section, I'll try to highlight the most popular items and give you some helpful tips for each. Much shellfish is sold live, which adds its own layer of challenge, but the rewards of truly fresh, well-prepared shellfish can't be beat.

Happily, a lot of the shellfish that we consume is in pretty good shape, both in terms of the environment and from a fish health standpoint. However, some glaring exceptions to this — such as shrimp — may require us to reconsider the way we think about and buy certain shellfish. Some great-tasting alternatives do exist, and although they might be a bit more expensive, I feel they're absolutely worth it.

There is something almost primitive about eating shellfish — the shells, the whole creatures, the simple preparations. I feel so connected to the ocean when I'm eating shellfish. And, of course, oysters, clams, and mussels do have a little seawater inside them. There is nothing better than cracking open a lobster on a deck overlooking the ocean, but we can come pretty darn close when we treat them right in our own backyard.

For advice on handling and storage, see page 277.

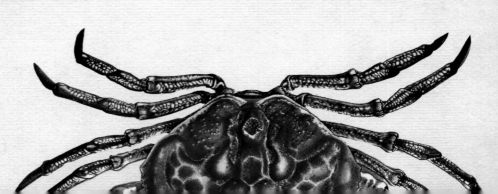

Bay Scallops

ORIGIN: *Eastern North America, China*

AVAILABILITY: *Year-round. Be aware of the potential for mislabelling, intentionally or unintentionally, due to the nature of the shellfish. Take care to ensure you get what you pay for.*

COMMON FORMS: *Shucked meat, raw, fresh, and frozen; occasionally live in-shell*

STOCK STATUS: *Wild harvest is decreasing, though well managed; farmed availability is good*

SOURCE: *Most North American catch is wild; many farmed variations come from Asia*

ALTERNATIVES: *Razor clams, sea scallops*

BAY SCALLOPS ARE a common variety of scallop that is sometimes served whole. Unfortunately, their point of origin is often unclear. All too frequently what you find labelled as "bay scallops" in grocery stores are not true "bays," and often come from countries with inadequate labelling standards, such as China. True bays come from the North American East Coast, from Nova Scotia and points south. They have lovely mauve/brown shells, with defined ridges emanating from the hinge, and are no more than 5 cm (2 inches) across. The meat, when shucked, is quite small compared to sea scallops, and bays run 40 to 60 count to a pound. For comparison, sea scallops run 16 to 20 count per pound, or more.

Because the meat yield is so low, the retail price for true bay scallops is quite high, often running north of $40 per pound. This, of course, tempts fishmongers into selling cheaper Chinese product, misleadingly labelled. True bay scallops are incredibly sweet when harvested from a well-managed fishery, or farmed responsibly, here in North America. They're a little pricier but worth every penny.

COUNT PER POUND

When buying shellfish, "count" refers to about how many of a specific shellfish are in a pound. Because the pieces are never all the same size, the count is always expressed as a range and is intended to provide the average size of the shellfish being sold. For example, 16/20 count shrimp will be of a size where there will be no less than 16 and no more than 20 shrimp per pound.

—CLAMS—

ORIGIN: *Worldwide*

AVAILABILITY: *Year-round*

COMMON FORMS: *Whole, live in-shell; shucked meat, fresh and frozen; and canned or bottled cooked clams*

STOCK STATUS: *Very good, no concern*

SOURCE: *Most of the catch is wild; some aquaculture clams are available, especially "pasta" and littleneck clams*

ALTERNATIVES: *mussels, oysters*

THERE ARE LITERALLY hundreds of species of clams throughout the world, many of which are commercially harvested. Not all of them have the same shelf life or flavour, or best method of handling. Of the thousands of varieties that exist, those that are routinely eaten by humans fall into two broad categories: hard-shell and soft-shell clams. Even within these two broad categories there are many varieties. The most obvious differences between hard- and soft-shell clams are, as their names suggest, the thickness and texture of their shells.

Hard-shell clams — such a quahogs, surf clams, and "pasta" clams — contain a bulbous, almost rubbery meat that is solidly attached to the hard shells. These clams tend to be somewhat round in shape and, when disturbed, close up tight, pulling all their body parts inside their protective enclave (so if your clam doesn't shut quickly when you tap on it, discard it). Bigger varieties take at least 10 minutes of heavy heat to cook and open up; smaller ones open a little quicker.

Soft-shell clams — such as steamers, long necks, and geoducks (pronounced *gooey-ducks*) — have rather thin and somewhat brittle shells with a rather obvious siphon protruding that can, but does not always, retract when disturbed. Most varieties are so fragile that they can easily be crushed between two fingers. Their meat is slight and quite delicate, and does not take more than a few minutes to cook. Soft-shell clams tend to release a considerable amount of liquid when cooked, so they can practically be steamed in their own "juices." The protruding siphon is covered by a dark sheath or "sock" that can taste quite bitter, so after cooking it is usually peeled off before the clam is eaten. An easy way to test for vitality when handling soft-shell clams is to touch the protruding siphon: if it retracts, the clam is alive; non-action suggests its demise.

Overall, I'd have to say that clams are my favourite shellfish. Many are harvested wild, typically hand-dug at low tide, though cultivation is a growing source of shellfish. Clams are very labour intensive but gentle on the environment and on the resource. Some of the most common wild clams include littlenecks, cherrystones, razor clams, mahogany clams, steamer clams, and geoducks. Cultivated varieties include Manila clams and "pasta" clams.

Can you eat raw clams? Yes! Many clams are delicious — and safe — to eat raw or briefly blanched. Littlenecks and cherrystones can be opened just like an oyster and eaten off the half shell. Razor clams can be removed from the shell with a paring knife and quickly cleaned, leaving only the white parts of the meat.

PASTA CLAMS

A "pasta clam" is a term for any number of small, hard-shell clams native to the Mediterranean and other warmer climates.

Geoducks — "the king of clams" — require a quick dip into a pot of boiling salted water, then shocking in ice water (see page 21). At this point, you can separate the siphon or "neck" from the rest of the clam with a sharp knife. Peel the "sock" or tough outer skin from the siphon, and thinly slice the beautiful white meat. Very tasty!

HOW TO CLEAN SOFT-SHELL CLAMS

Some clams, such as steamers and savoury clams, require "purging" — or soaking — to remove naturally occurring sand. I've heard of many tricks, but the most effective method is to make a very light saltwater brine (about 250 mL/1 cup non-iodized salt mixed into 4 L/16 cups cold water), and then to immerse the clams in it, keeping them chilled. You will need to change the water a couple of times — always using salt water — and it will take about a day of purging to get rid of the bulk of the sand. Littleneck clams, cherrystones, razor clams, and Manila clams typically don't require this step. It is important to note that clams purchased at fish shops have almost always been purged before they are brought to market. If you have harvested clams from shore yourself or bought them from a clam digger before they have been brought to the pound for purging, however, you will need to purge them.

— STUFFIES —

When I was making regular trips to Boston and Rhode Island in the United States,
I came upon these delicious baked clams. They're totally addictive — especially the Rhode Island
version, which is served with chorizo. You can make them ahead of time and refrigerate
for a couple days, then simply heat to serve.

30 live cherrystone clams, rinsed

5 mL (1 tsp) vegetable oil

2 links mild or hot chorizo (your choice),
  casings removed, chopped

2 stalks celery, diced

1 medium onion, diced

1 red bell pepper, seeded and diced

250 mL (1 cup) plain breadcrumbs

30 to 45 g (1 to 1.5 oz.) picked fresh
  thyme leaves

Zest and juice of 1 lemon

150 mL (⅔ cup) finely grated
  Parmesan cheese

Black pepper, to taste

Fill a large pot with a tight-fitting lid with about 2.5 cm (1 inch) of water. Cover with the lid and bring to a boil over high heat. When the water starts to boil, put all clams in the pot. Let steam for 3 minutes, and then stir. Cover and continue to cook for another 4 to 5 minutes (for a total of 7 to 8 minutes). Using a slotted spoon or tongs, transfer clams that have opened to a large bowl. If any are still closed, cook for an additional 2 to 3 minutes. Remove pot from heat, transfer open clams to the bowl, and discard any remaining clams that have not opened. Discard cooking liquid. Set bowl of clams aside until cool enough to handle.

Using your fingers or an oyster knife or sturdy table knife, split the cooked shells in half and transfer clam meat to a chopping board, reserving shells. Roughly chop clam meat, and set aside. Clean 30 of the shell halves and arrange open-side up on a baking sheet; set sheet aside. Discard remaining shells.

In a sauté pan over medium-low heat, heat oil. Add chorizo, celery, onion, and bell pepper. Cover and cook, stirring occasionally, until vegetables have softened, 10 to 12 minutes. Remove pan from heat, drain excess oil, and let cool.

In a medium bowl, combine chopped clam meat, cooked chorizo mixture, breadcrumbs, thyme, and lemon juice. Stir well. Using a spoon, divide mixture evenly between the clean half shells. Sprinkle each with a little lemon zest, a lot of cheese, and maybe a crack of black pepper. Place the oven rack in the second-from-the-top position and preheat oven to 230°C (450°F). Broil clams for 6 to 8 minutes, until tops are browned. (If after 6 minutes or so the clams aren't browning enough, raise them closer to the heat.)

Expect each person to eat 6 to 10 clams, unless they are a soulless robot.

FRIED STEAMER CLAMS

Outside of lobster rolls, the number-one menu item people look for when they visit the Maritimes is fried clams. Sadly, nowadays, most places serve a pre-battered catastrophe called a "slam strip," which consists of surf clams, breaded and frozen somewhere on Earth, shipped by a large multinational distributor, and fried with no care or concern until they vaguely resemble what might have once been a clam. Truly great fried clams require the right clam, the right batter, and the right amount of respect. With this recipe, you can make your own.

1 kg (2 lb) live steamer (soft-shell) clams, purged thoroughly (see page 12)

150 mL (⅔ cup) all-purpose flour

150 mL (⅔ cup) fine corn flour

7 mL (1½ tsp) baking powder

5 mL (1 tsp) salt

200 mL (¾ cup + 5 tsp) light-flavoured beer or soda water

15 g (0.5 oz) picked fresh thyme leaves

3 L (12 cups) vegetable oil

Fill a large pot with a tight-fitting lid with ½ inch of water. Cover with the lid and bring to a boil over high heat. When the water starts to boil, carefully place all clams in the pot. Cover and cook until clams have opened widely and firmed up a bit, about 10 minutes. Discard any clams that didn't open. Strain cooking liquid, let cool, and save for another day; it will keep for at least 4 days in the fridge (steamer "clam juice" is the most versatile and delicious clam juice — perfect for chowders and pasta dishes).

Using your fingers, pluck out the clam meat. Pull off the "socks" (the black skin covering the siphons) and discard. Place clams on a baking sheet lined with paper towel and set aside to dry until ready to use.

In a shallow bowl, combine flours, baking powder, and salt. Slowly whisk in beer or soda and mix just until smooth (don't overmix, as you want to retain some of the fizziness). Stir in thyme. Set aside.

In a medium pot, heat vegetable oil to 180°C (350°F).

Using a fork, dip clams, one by one, first into the batter and then into the hot oil. Work in small batches, perhaps 6 clams at a time. Fry each batch for 3 to 4 minutes. Using a slotted spoon or spider, transfer fried clams to a platter lined in paper towel. Repeat until all clams have been cooked.

Serve hot, with lemon.

Serves 4 as an appetizer

INSIDE A CLAM-PACKING PLANT

Back in the day, packing plants dotted the shores of Atlantic Canada. (In the Maritimes, shellfish packing began on a large scale in the mid 19th century, and although it's still a vital industry in some places, it began to dwindle in scale by the late 1970s.) Canned fish, lobster, chicken, and beef were all common, but the most popular canned item was clams. As with other labour-intensive industries, many of the canneries have now left North America for Asia. Happily, a few holdouts are still doing things the traditional way.

   David and Carla Annand operate Canada's only clam-processing facility, Annand Clams, in Conway, Prince Edward Island. Bar clams are one of the largest clams commonly fished and require processing before they can be consumed. The Annands start by steaming open the heavy shells and then pulling out the whole clam meat. They then separate the clam meat into its main components: the adductor muscle, the "foot," and the "strip" or "mantle." You might be familiar with clam foot if you've ever eaten *hokkigai* (clam nigiri) at a sushi bar, which typically uses the foot of a similar clam, Stimpson's surf clam (also known as the Arctic surf clam). The bar clam foot is white/beige, unlike the Arctic surf clam, which has a red tinge but is

otherwise indistinguishable in taste and texture. The Annands bottle their bar clams, and use the strips and adductor muscles for making fried clams, a breaded favourite of many Maritimers (see page 17).

It's difficult to automate much of the processing, so a dedicated, hardworking staff is key to the Annands' operation. I support keeping this type of processing as local as possible, and encourage everyone to read the labels on their canned clams carefully. Many seemingly "local" clams are, in fact, packed thousands of miles away.

Above: Clam strips ready for breading and frying.
Right: Bottled bar clams.

SHAVED GEODUCK SIPHON WITH LIME AND OLIVE OIL

Geoduck (pronounced "gooey duck") is a West Coast clam with a shell that ranges from 12 to 25 cm across, and a siphon that can extend at least that far outside of the shell. They look and feel completely alien. Much of what is between the shells is not super tasty. It's best to target the sweet meat from the siphon.

2 L (8 cups) water
100 mL (6 tbsp + 2 tsp) salt
1 live geoduck
Zest and juice of 2 limes
High-quality olive oil
Finishing salt (light flakes, not iodized)

In a large pot, bring water to a rolling boil. Add salt. Plunge the whole clam into the boiling water and cook for 1 minute. Using tongs, remove clam and rinse under cold running water, or submerge in a bowl of ice water to stop the cooking and make it cool enough to handle. Let drain and pat clam dry.

Separate the clam meat from the shell: Insert a paring knife between the shell and the body at the base of the neck. Run the knife all the way around the top edge of the shell, being careful to cut through the adductor muscles holding the shell and body together. Pry the shell off and behold the insides of the clam. Cut away and discard the dark, oval-shaped stomach. If you like, you can trim off the yellowish-white part of the clam "body" (the part that rests inside the shell) and save it for chowder or pasta. Here, though, we will set it aside and concentrate on the siphon.

Cut the siphon from the clam body, just above where the siphon ends. Now peel off the brown "sock" (outer skin): Using your hands, firmly hold the cut end of the siphon and, in one fluid motion, peel away the tough skin (the sock will be surprisingly long); discard the sock. Cut the siphon lengthwise, rinse thoroughly, and pat dry. Wrap it well in plastic wrap and freeze for 4 to 5 hours, until it is quite firm.

Remove the clam from the freezer and discard plastic wrap. Using a meat slicer or a very sharp knife, and starting from the wide end of the siphon, cut as many thin slices as you can. Where the meat starts to turn colour slightly, stop slicing.

Arrange slices on many small serving plates or one large one. Spoon lime juice over them, and then drizzle with a little olive oil. Finish with salt. Serve as soon as you can, even with a bit of frost still on them.

Serves 8 to 10 as a snack or 4 to 6, plated, as an appetizer

RAZOR CLAMS WITH GARLIC AND HERBS

Very tricky to capture in the wild, the razor clam will fool you with its speed and dig deep into the sand. Once in hand, though, they are among the sweetest clams around — very tender and very easy to prepare. In North America, most commercial harvests occur in the American Northeast. There are two main varieties: the Atlantic jackknife (the most common long clam) and the stout razor. Both are equally delicious and can be prepared in the same manner.

200 mL (¾ cup + 5 tsp) olive oil

6 cloves garlic, minced

2 shallots, minced

2 ancho (dried poblano) or similar
   mild chilies, seeded and minced

100 mL (6 tbsp + 2 tsp) dry white wine

12 live razor clams, purged thoroughly
   (see page 12)

100 mL (6 tbsp + 2 tsp) picked fresh
   tarragon leaves

In a medium sauté pan, over low heat, combine olive oil, garlic, shallots, and chilies. Cover and cook for about 10 minutes, stirring occasionally. Add wine, and increase heat to high. When mixture starts to bubble rapidly, add clams. Cover and steam clams for 3 to 4 minutes. Stir gently to ensure even heat. Cover again, and steam for an additional 4 to 5 minutes. Using tongs or a slotted spoon, transfer clams to a platter (discard any that have not opened). Return pan to heat, and cook liquid until reduced by half. Remove pan from heat, and stir in tarragon. Spoon a little of the sauce over each clam, and serve.

Serves 4 as an appetizer

Do Not Attempt a Clambake

You may have heard of this semi-mythical feast. Sometimes referred to as a "lobster bake," the concept is the same: Find a beach, dig a pit, line it with rocks, and light a big fire. While the coals are building, gather small sacks of clams and mussels, a bunch of live lobsters, and a little seaweed. Get some corn and perhaps some potatoes, maybe some sausage, and a big piece of burlap. Once you've deemed the coals sufficiently hot, start laying everything into the pit: some seaweed, the lobsters and shellfish, the vegetables and sausage, a bit more seaweed, and then cover it all with the burlap that has been dunked in the picturesque ocean to help generate steam. Weigh the cloth down with rocks, start shucking some oysters, and have a few beers while waiting the hour and a half for everything to cook. When the moment of truth arrives, the pitmaster rolls back the burlap and voilá: a feast for kings and queens. Sounds amazing, right? Wrong. Don't ever try this.

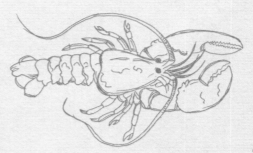

Among the many potential challenges:

- Digging a pit deep enough
- Bringing enough wood
- Failing to account for the ambient temperature of the sand — a beach in July and a beach in September are very different things
- Transporting everything to and from the cook site: the cord of wood, coolers of shellfish and other food, ice, drinks, garbage cans, chairs, etc. (and don't forget to bring flashlights, since you'll be cleaning up in the dark)
- What if everything goes wrong? What if you don't get the lobsters cooked? Do you have a backup heat source? What if it rains?

In short, there are so many potential pitfalls that I am not sure why anyone would try — except for the fact that if all does go right, it can be the most delicious and memorable dinner you've ever had.

I've done many and consider myself a pretty good clambake cook, but even I've been the victim of my own hubris. When we opened Joe Beef in Montreal, I pitched Fred and Dave on the idea of a clambake in the back alley. What an idiot. It was fall, so by the time service started it was dark. I pulled some cars and trucks around back to shine their lights on me so that I could see. And then it started to rain.

Naturally, our clambake dinner was a pretty popular dish that night: "Two clambakes, four clambakes, two more, three more . . ." If you've ever worked in a restaurant, you know the feeling of not being ready when service starts. Not only was I not ready, I wasn't even close. Less than fifteen minutes before service was to begin, I knew it was going to be a disaster. We quickly started cooking the separate items in the kitchen, trying to do it that way. It was sad. I took it off the menu after first service and licked my wounds. It's something we can laugh at now, but at the time, when Joe Beef was so new, it felt like a failure.

I have since developed foolproof strategies for creating a clambake experience at home, but it still requires a pretty big barbecue—much bigger than what I had that night.

Backyard Clambake for Twenty

If you must.

500 mL (2 cups) salt
20 live lobsters
4.5 kg (10 lb) baby potatoes
10 whole fennel bulbs, quartered
2 kg (4 lb) mild sausage, cut into chunks
10 cobs corn, husked and halved
1 to 2 kg (2 to 4 lb) live mussels,
   scrubbed and debearded
1 to 2 kg (2 to 4 lb) live littleneck clams,
   scrubbed
2 kg (4 lb) butter
50 to 60 live oysters, for serving

Equipment
Small shovel
14 to 18 kg (30 to 40 lb) charcoal
5 to 7 chunks (10 to 15 lb) hardwood
   (avoid logs, as they take too long to
   turn to coals)
10 rectangular aluminum pans
   (lasagna-style), about 41 × 36 × 9 cm
   (16 × 14 × 4 inches) with lids
2 large pots, with lids
3 to 4 large sheet pans, to cover
   coal bed

Dig a bed for your coals, about 1.8 m long × 0.9 m wide × 0.6 m deep (6 ft × 3 ft × 2 ft). Depth is very important. Pour in half the charcoal, distribute it evenly, and light it. Let it burn down before gradually adding chunks of wood and more charcoal to keep the temperature steady.

Meanwhile, fill the sink with cold water and add at least a couple of cups of salt. Bring a large pot of salted water to a rolling boil (the water should taste like the ocean). Working in batches if needed, plunge the lobsters into the boiling water and cook for 8 to 10 minutes. Using tongs, immediately immerse lobsters in the salted cold-water bath. Once the lobsters have cooled, drain and set aside.

At the same time, in another large pot of boiling water, cook the potatoes for 10 to 15 minutes, until tender. Drain and rinse under cold running water. Set aside.

Arrange the aluminum pans side by side and evenly divide fennel, sausage, corn, mussels, clams, and butter among them. Split the cooked lobsters in half, and nestle 4 halves into each pan, along with some potatoes. The pans will be quite full. Cover each with a lid, and then poke small holes all over the sides and tops to let in smoke (aim for about 15 holes per pan).

Shovel the hot coals to the edges of the coal bed, and arrange 5 or 6 pans side by side in their place. Top with the remaining pans — two layers of pans is best. Once all pans are in, evenly distribute the remaining charcoal all around. Cover the sheet pans entirely with coals. Let cook, covered, for about 30 minutes.

Shuck some oysters for your friends, while waiting.

After half an hour, pull one pan from the coals. Open it, to check on status. As long as most of the clams and mussels are steamed open, you're good to go. If not, put the pan back in for another 15 minutes or so, keeping covered. One container feeds two people.

Sure, it's not oceanside, but you'll still get that wonderful smoke/steam flavour. It'll be a memorable evening, for sure. Enjoy!

COCKLES

ORIGIN: *Worldwide*
AVAILABILITY: *Year-round*
COMMON FORMS: *Whole, live in-shell; shucked meat, fresh and frozen*
STOCK STATUS: *Very good, no concern*
SOURCE: *All catch is wild*
ALTERNATIVES: *clams, oysters*

COCKLES ARE NOT clams, but they're often confused with them. They are seen less in North America than in Europe and Asia, though they are native to the North American West Coast, and can be found on the East Coast. The shells are typically ridged and look like a cross between a clam and a scallop. There are over 200 varieties of cockles worldwide, but not all are edible. Some are surprisingly tiny, such as berbigão cockles from Portugal, which are no bigger than a fingertip, 40 to 50 per pound (unlike traditional littleneck clams, which are about 9 per pound). Other outstanding varieties include the New Zealand cockle, which has a beautiful greenish shell and an intense brininess, and the blood clam, which isn't a true cockle but shares most traits. Blood clams stand out because they contain hemoglobin, which makes their blood look red. When these clams are shucked raw, they look as if they are bleeding. Not to everyone's taste, but delicious, nonetheless.

Cockles, like clams, can sometimes be sandy. If you open a test cockle and find some sand, do not worry. Make a simple brine of 250 mL (1 cup) of non-iodized salt mixed into 3 to 4 L (12 to 16 cups) of water. Put cockles in the brine and refrigerate for 3 to 4 hours. Remove cockles, make a fresh brine, and repeat. It can be a bit of a pain, but it can be done in two stages; just keep them refrigerated in the meantime.

—CRAB—

DUNGENESS, KING, ROCK, STONE, SNOW, BLUE, JONAH

ORIGIN: *Worldwide*

AVAILABILITY: *Year-round, though each species has its own season*

COMMON FORMS: *Whole, live or cooked; whole, frozen raw; cooked meat; raw frozen sections; canned crab is available but is the least desirable as it is often of low grade and mixed with other fish products — avoid all cheaply priced canned meat*

STOCK STATUS: *Extremely dependent on species and country of origin; North America is a safe bet*

SOURCE: *All catch is wild*

ALTERNATIVES: *lobster, langoustine*

DUNGENESS, KING, ROCK, stone, snow, blue, and Jonah crabs are merely the most important species in North America. Other varieties include the spider, mud, horse, brown, and more. They are popular in other regions but less likely to be encountered here. In fact, two types — the horse crab and flower crab — account for over 500,000 tons fished annually, of which we see almost none.

As with any other high-value fishery, there are generally strong management systems in place in North America for crab. In fact, almost all seven of these crab varieties are good choices, with strong populations and minimally impactful harvest methods. Two primary exceptions are Atlantic rock crab and Canadian-fished Jonah crab, which is caught incidentally in the lobster fishery and thus potentially more exploited than official figures show. Still, for the most part, you are safe picking up any crab fished in the United States or Canada.

The same cannot be said for shellfish coming from Russia, India, Argentina, and Vietnam. Various problems exist with these fisheries, from poor or non-existent management, to high levels of bycatch, to outright fraud. According to Seafood Watch: "It's impossible to know when any species of crab is caught legally because supply chain information isn't reliable. Russia doesn't acknowledge that it exports crab to the U.S., only to Korea and Japan. In 2013, an estimated

To make the sauce: In a saucepan, over low heat, combine oil and shallots. Cook, stirring occasionally, for about 10 minutes, until the shallots are translucent and soft. Increase heat to high, and add white wine. Cook until reduced by half, 10 to 12 minutes. Reduce heat to medium, and stir in crab "butter" and cream. Cook for 5 to 8 minutes, until sauce has thickened. Add salt and pepper, to taste.

Serve crab with "butter" sauce on the side.

Allow 1 crab per person. Makes enough sauce for 6 people. If you are serving more people, adjust quantities accordingly.

If you've got company in the kitchen, one person can work on cleaning and cracking the crabs, while another makes the crab "butter" sauce.

SNOW CRAB BALLS

A lighter version of crab cakes, snow crab balls start with a sort of béchamel paste, which largely melts away during deep-frying. Highly addictive.

For the béchamel sauce:

125 mL (½ cup) unsalted butter

125 mL (½ cup) all-purpose flour

500 mL (2 cups) whole milk, warmed slightly

Salt and pepper, to taste

For the balls:

60 mL (¼ cup) butter

8 shallots, finely chopped

800 g (28 oz) picked crab meat

400 mL (1⅔ cups) béchamel sauce (recipe above)

100 mL (6 tbsp + 2 tsp) freshly grated Parmesan (or Pecorino) cheese

2 eggs

675 mL (2¾ cups) plain panko crumbs

Lemon wedges, for serving

To make the sauce: In a saucepan, over medium heat, melt butter. Whisk in flour and cook, whisking constantly, until mixture achieves a light golden colour, about 10 minutes. Remove pan from heat and let cool to just above room temperature.

Once cool, return pan to low heat and whisk in warm milk. Simmer for 5 minutes, stirring occasionally. Strain through a fine-mesh sieve into a bowl to remove any lumps (discard solids). Add salt and pepper, to taste. Set aside.

To make the crab balls: In a saucepan, over low heat, melt butter. Add shallots and cook, stirring occasionally, for about 10 minutes, until the shallots are translucent and soft. Remove pan from heat and let cool.

In a bowl, combine crab, cooled shallot mixture, béchamel sauce, and Parmesan, and stir well. The mixture should be thick enough that you can shape it into light balls. If not, add more cheese. Set aside.

In a shallow bowl, whisk eggs. Place panko in another shallow bowl. Line a baking sheet with parchment paper. Using your hands, form crab mixture into 2- to 3-cm (¾- to 1¼-inch) balls. Roll each ball in egg, and then in the panko. Place on prepared baking sheet.

In a large pot or deep-fryer, heat oil to 180°C (350°F). Working in batches, fry balls for about 5 minutes, until golden. Serve with lemon wedges.

Makes about 24 balls, enough for 6 appetizers

CRAWFISH

ORIGIN: *Worldwide*
AVAILABILITY: *Year-round; live crawfish mostly from February to September*
COMMON FORMS: *Whole, live; whole, frozen; picked tail meat*
STOCK STATUS: *Good, little concern*
SOURCE: *All catch is wild, though usually from controlled areas*
ALTERNATIVES: *shrimp, langoustine*

THESE SMALL FRESHWATER lobsters found under rocks the world over have been a cost-effective snack for ages. In fact, crawfish (also known as "crayfish") are the number-one shellfish product in the United States, by pounds. But we see them less and less in Canada, which is a shame. The season for fresh crawfish typically runs February through September. On the West Coast, especially in Oregon, you can find them until November/December; they are a different species, the "signal" crawfish, so named for the white spot on their claw that evokes an old-time railway signal flag.

Oftentimes, you will find crawfish precooked and frozen, which is still pretty tasty, though commonly from China, which can be problematic. To "refresh" frozen crawfish, simply steam them in a pot for 8 to 10 minutes. Precooked products are typically seasoned, so there's no need to do much to them. Chinese imports have displaced much U.S. frozen product, which has hurt packing plants down South. Tariffs are being introduced to try to correct the imbalance.

STUFFED CRAWFISH "BITS" OVER RICE

If you have leftover crawfish from your festive boil (see next page), this is where to turn.
I recommend preparing the crawfish in New Orleans during Jazz Fest, but it's not required.

2 to 2.5 kg (4 to 5.5 lb) whole crawfish (fresh or frozen), cooked (see next page)

250 mL (1 cup) butter

1 large onion, diced

1 green bell pepper, seeded and diced

425 mL (1¾ cups) plain breadcrumbs

10 whole tomatoes, peeled and roughly chopped

250 mL (1 cup) your favourite barbecue sauce

560 mL (2¼ cups) long-grain rice

Grab the head firmly in one hand, and the tail firmly in the other, and twist and pull the tail from each crawfish. Using your fingers, remove the meat from the tail sections and set aside. Hollow out the crawfish heads by simply pulling the legs and attached viscera from outer shell; reserve the heads for making bisque. Using a sharp knife, finely chop the crawfish tail meat.

In a skillet over medium-low heat, melt butter. Sauté onion and peppers for 15 minutes, until softened. Remove pan from heat. Add breadcrumbs and tail meat, and stir together to form a paste. Carefully spoon mixture into each reserved crawfish head, until just full.

In a shallow pan over medium-low heat, combine tomatoes and barbecue sauce. Arrange stuffed crawfish heads, stuffing-side up, in pan. Let simmer for 20 to 30 minutes, until sauce has thickened slightly.

Meanwhile, cook rice according to the package instructions and keep warm.

To serve, place a scoop of rice onto each serving plate, and spoon crawfish and sauce overtop (about 6 crawfish per person).

Serves 8 as a hearty appetizer or 4 as a main course

COOKING LIVE CRAWFISH

When buying live crawfish, you will find that some of them are, inevitably, dead. This is normal, and they are still fine to cook as long as there is no putrid smell coming from them (it's safe to presume that the whole batch was living when shipped and some died during transport). As live crawfish are rarely available, it's likely that the fishmonger would have brought them in as a special order, which means the packing and shipping date would not be more than a couple of days. Note there is no need to purge crawfish purchased commercially; they arrive at fish shops already clean.

To cook live crawfish, fill a large pot one-quarter full of water. Toss in some quartered onions, garlic cloves, celery, bay leaves, cayenne pepper, chunks of lemon, hot sauce, and salt. Get the pot to a rolling boil, and fill halfway with crawfish. Cover, and boil for 7 to 8 minutes, turning them once to ensure they get well seasoned. Drain, and serve. Allow 15 to 20 crawfish per person.

Eating crawfish is very much a hands-on procedure. The easiest and tastiest way is to pinch and pull the head off. The base of the head contains a tasty bit of innards, so sucking on the back of the head will result in a little treat. Then you can simply use your hands to pull apart the remaining tail section and suck out the flesh.

—Langoustines—

ORIGIN: *Northeast Atlantic*

AVAILABILITY: *Year-round, though each species has its own season*

COMMON FORMS: *Whole, live or cooked; whole, frozen raw; cooked meat; frozen raw sections*

STOCK STATUS: *Extremely dependent on species and country of origin; North America is a safe bet*

SOURCE: *All catch is wild*

ALTERNATIVES: *crawfish, crab, prawns*

"SCAMPI" IN ITALY, "Norway lobster" in the United Kingdom, and "langoustines" in France and North America — no matter what you call them, they look like tiny mutant lobsters and taste like sweet shrimp. Scotland provides a huge percentage of the worldwide catch, which is 100 percent wild and pretty well managed, mostly due to their burrowing habits, which make them difficult to capture. Only the tail meat is eaten; the head and claws are discarded.

They aren't readily available in North America but can sometimes be found fresh. The frozen version is totally acceptable and much more reliably found.

HOW TO COOK LANGOUSTINES

To clean langoustines, it's best to leave them whole with the head and appendages intact. Using a sharp knife, split them down the back of the shell and remove any dark intestine. For recipes that call for only the meat, it's easier and quicker to cut off the head and pull off the legs, then split the back and clean out the intestine before cooking (they cook a little quicker this way, in about 3 minutes). If using frozen langoustines, let them thaw out in the fridge before cooking.

To cook langoustines, bring a large pot of well-salted water to a rolling boil. It certainly doesn't hurt to add a few bay leaves, quartered onion, roughly chopped carrot, and some loose fresh parsley. Plunge the langoustines into the pot and cook for 4 to 5 minutes. Serve right away, with a bit of garlic butter on the side. A bit of work is involved to extract the meat, but consider it a conversation starter.

LANGOUSTINE RAVIOLI

*The average langoustine doesn't yield a lot of meat, so using it as a filling
for ravioli is a good way to stretch the flavour and use the whole crustacean.*

For the pasta dough:

325 mL (1⅓ cups) all-purpose flour

2 whole eggs + 1 egg yolk, beaten

Water, if needed

For the filling and sauce:

12 fresh whole langoustines

60 mL (¼ cup) butter

60 mL (¼ cup) oil

2 shallots, minced

1 carrot, diced

400 mL (1⅔ cups) water

2 stalks celery, peeled and diced

100 g (3.5 oz) peeled fava beans

50 mL (3 tbsp + 1 tsp) heavy or
   whipping (35%) cream

Salt and pepper, to taste

30 g (1 oz) tarragon leaves

To make the dough: In a large bowl, combine flour and eggs until the mixture comes together to form a dough. Using your hands, knead dough until it forms a smooth ball. If the mixture is a little dry, gradually knead in tiny amounts of water until you achieve the desired consistency. Cover tightly in plastic wrap, and let rest for at least 30 to 60 minutes.

Clean the langoustines: Separate the tails from the bodies by gently yet firmly pulling the head from the body, twisting slightly. To remove the tail meat, break the tail between the third and fourth segment (the tail has six segments total), gently twist the middle joint to break the shell, and then gently pull away the tail end; the remaining segments can then be peeled off easily. If you do it right, the intestine will pull off with the tail end. Set tail meat aside; reserve shells.

To make the stock: In a skillet, over medium heat, melt butter with oil. Add shallots and carrot, and cook, stirring occasionally, for about 10 minutes, until softened. Add water and reserved langoustine shells. Reduce heat and simmer for 20 to 30 minutes. Strain mixture through a fine-mesh sieve into a saucepan; discard shells. Set aside.

To make the ravioli: Put a large pot of salted water on to boil.

Roll out dough until paper thin (just under 2 mm/1⁄16 inch). Cut into twenty-four 6-cm (2½-inch) circles. Place one piece of langoustine tail meat in the centre of each of 12 circles, and season with a little salt and pepper. Brush the edges of the pasta with water, and cover with the remaining circles. Pinch edges well to seal. Cook ravioli in boiling salted water for 4 to 5 minutes.

To finish the sauce: Meanwhile, bring reserved stock to a simmer over medium heat. Add celery, and cook for 5 minutes. Add fava beans, and cook for 5 minutes. Stir in cream. Add a touch of salt and pepper, to taste. Increase heat to high and simmer for 3 to 5 minutes. Remove pan from heat and stir in tarragon.

Divide the sauce between your serving plates and top with ravioli. Drizzle with olive oil. Serve immediately.

Serves 4 as an appetizer or 2 as a main course

LOBSTER

ORIGIN: *Worldwide*

AVAILABILITY: *Year-round*

COMMON FORMS: *Whole, live or cooked; whole, frozen raw; cooked meat; frozen raw sections*

STOCK STATUS: *Very dependent on origin; North American and European products have excellent management; other fisheries such as Caribbean lobster are working toward management plans*

SOURCE: *All catch is wild*

ALTERNATIVES: *langoustine, crab*

SOMETIMES REFERRED TO as the "cockroach of the sea" or just "bug," few fish have risen as high in value over the years as lobster. Some Maritime residents still insist that they were sent to school with lobster sandwiches and were mocked for them, as it suggested their family was poor and backward. Personally, I feel these tales are a little exaggerated, but it's definitely true that for a long time lobster fishing wasn't a very lucrative chore. It's also true that there are many misconceptions and myths about these tasty creatures — so many, in fact, that I've decided to include some of the more common (and outlandish) claims here for easy reference. In no particular order:

LOBSTERS SCREAM WHEN YOU THROW THEM IN THE POT.

Not true. I've cooked tens of thousands of lobsters in my life, and not one has emitted so much as a sigh.

FEMALE LOBSTERS TASTE BETTER.

Again, not true. Females contain roe, which is an added bonus if you enjoy that sort of thing, but the meat is identical.

HARD-SHELL LOBSTERS ARE SUPERIOR.

True. The harder the shell, the less water content in the muscle, and the fuller your meat will be. Hard-shell lobsters are more easily found from September through to the end of June.

BIG LOBSTERS ARE TOUGHER.

Nah, it's all in how you cook them. Sure, a big lobster will be a bit stringy but not tougher. Lots of folks insist on 500 g (1 lb) lobsters (or even smaller!). Personally, I look for a lobster around 1.5 kg (3 lb) — more meat in the body and better bang for your buck.

IF A LOBSTER DIES BEFORE YOU COOK IT, IT WON'T BE ANY GOOD.

Not necessarily true. Of course, cook it as soon as you can, but if the tail curls up and is still "springy," the lobster is fine. They do break down quickly after dying, but it's not instantaneous.

YOU NEED TO KILL THE LOBSTER WITH A NEEDLE, OR SOME SUCH METHOD, BEFORE COOKING IT.

Nope. In my experience, the most humane way to go about it is to use the biggest pot you have, get the water to a fast rolling boil, and plunge the lobster in headfirst. It will die very quickly. Too many folks use too small a pot, and when they put the lobster into the water, it cools the water down too much, and the lobster thrashes around for an inordinate amount of time.

LOBSTERS FEEL PAIN.

Well, I'm not sure why this is even discussed, as we know that all the other animals we eat feel pain, and it (mostly) doesn't change our eating habits. Using the boiling technique above will limit the amount of anguish for all concerned. There has been much study about lobsters and pain receptors, and the results are inconclusive. My understanding has always been that they don't have the ability to feel pain the way we do, but this may be proven wrong someday. In any case, try to minimize the suffering.

Now that we have that out of the way, we can talk about the creatures themselves.

Very strict management has meant a stable lobster population, and the method of catching — by trap — is completely selective and gentle, ensuring that both the environment and other species aren't harmed by lobster catches. It is almost impossible to determine the age of a lobster, as they shed their entire skeleton in order to grow larger, but it's thought that the smallest allowed — roughly 500 g (1 lb) — lobsters are 5 to 7 years old. Some jurisdictions have a maximum size as well, allowing more prolific older females to continue to do their thing.

COOKING LOBSTER

Typically, a 500 g (1 lb) lobster will yield 90 to 125 g (3 to 4 oz) of meat, so be aware that your truly hungry guests might require something in the 750 g to 1 kg (1½ to 2 lb) category. If you have a good, large pot and suitable burner, a 500 g (1 lb) lobster will take 6 to 9 minutes to cook from the time the water returns to a boil, depending on the hardness of the shell. For lobsters that are 750 g to 1 kg (1½ to 2 lb), allow 9 to 15 minutes. For 1 to 1.5 kg (2 to 3 lb), allow 12 to 20 minutes. After that, add about 5 minutes per 500 g (1 lb), to a maximum of 25 to 30 minutes. For truly large lobsters, kill them in the boiling water, remove the claws, and make a small incision in the body, behind the eyes. The claws will take about 20 minutes to cook, and the body about 5 minutes longer.

— LATE SUMMER LOBSTER — AND AWESOME TOMATO SALAD

To be honest, this salad only works for about two months of the year — July and August — when tomatoes are at their finest. Also, it's really nice to eat this one outdoors, preferably seaside. Simplicity and high-quality ingredients are key here. If you pre-shuck your lobster, it will dry out. If you use mediocre olive oil, it will ruin the dish. If the tomatoes aren't on point, they won't give off any juice to add to the dressing.

2 lobsters, boiled and chilled

Zest and juice of 1 lemon

5 mL (1 tsp) apple cider vinegar

20 mL (4 tsp) granulated sugar

4 medium or 2 large very nice tomatoes (try to use a mix of colours)

High-quality olive oil

Arugula shoots (or other peppery shoots, such as radish) or baby arugula (not as good, really)

Finishing salt (light flakes, not iodized) and cracked black pepper, to taste

Using your hands, twist the tails and claws from the lobsters. Gently crack the claws and pull out the meat, trying to keep it as intact as possible (the larger claw has a hard piece in the meat, right at the joint, so be sure to pull that out; the smaller claw doesn't have this same bit). For the tail, first ensure that the end that was attached to the body is clean. If it is a bit slimy, green, or black, that's totally fine. Just get a small pot of salted water boiling, and then dip the end in quickly, shaking it around a little. (In a pinch, you can run it under hot tap water.) Once clean, using a sharp knife, cut the tail lengthwise. You may see a dark line running the length of the meat. If so, pull it out with your fingers. Remove the tail meat and cut it into sections, roughly emulating the natural sections of the tail. Set the lobster meat aside.

In a small bowl, combine lemon zest and juice, vinegar, and sugar. Set aside.

Cut tomatoes into different shapes and sizes. Follow the creases and contours of the tomatoes. Variety is key. Scatter tomatoes loosely on an oval platter.

Place chunks of lobster meat among the tomato, and spoon the vinaigrette all over, trying to touch everything with at least a drop or two. Working in a spiral, from the centre outward, drizzle a nice amount of olive oil on the plate. Garnish with arugula shoots, and season with salt and pepper. Serve.

Serves 4 as a family-style appetizer or 2 as a main course, individually plated

Mantis Prawns

ORIGIN: *Mediterranean, Southeast Asia*
AVAILABILITY: *Year-round, mostly September through June*
COMMON FORMS: *Whole, fresh*
STOCK STATUS: *Good overall; little concern*
SOURCE: *All catch is wild*
ALTERNATIVES: *shrimp, langoustine*

Mantis shrimp, mantis prawn, and *Squilla mantis* are all names for a creature you probably haven't seen in many fish shops, though this should change, as they are truly delicious and not over-exploited. Most commercial fisheries exist in the Mediterranean and Eastern Atlantic, though they are fished in Malaysia as well. A related species has been found off the East Coast of North America, though there hasn't yet been sufficient commercial demand for them to start a proper fishery, which is a shame.

The flavour of the meat is reminiscent of both lobster and shrimp. Mantis prawns are easy to prepare, and their shells make an excellent stock. They are typically sold fresh, and can be put on a skewer and simply grilled. Or, just as easily, they can be sautéed quickly (4 to 5 minutes, turning frequently) and served hot. I recommend cooking them in the shell and having your guests peel them as they go. This way, they get to suck on the delicious juices that hide in the nooks and crannies of their fabulous shells.

Mussels

ORIGIN: *Worldwide*

AVAILABILITY: *Year-round, though in summer the mussels are "weaker" and tend to have a shorter shelf life, with smaller meats*

COMMON FORMS: *Whole, live in-shell; frozen, in-shell and half-shell*

STOCK STATUS: *Very good, no concern*

SOURCE: *Most North American catch is cultivated; European harvest is mixed, though rarely seen here; New Zealand greenshells are farmed, though seed is mostly wild*

ALTERNATIVES: *clams, especially Manila, savoury, and littleneck*

MUSSELS ARE ONE of the best values in the seafood world — so inexpensive and flexible. Yet, until 30 years ago, they were almost unheard of in North America. Spain and China are the largest producers worldwide, at about 800 million pounds annually. Canada lags far behind, with 40 million pounds a year. And the United States is even further back, at 10 million pounds, give or take. Nonetheless, North American mussels are uniformly high quality. The West Coast focuses on the gallo mussel, while *edulis* dominates the East. Gallo mussels tend to be larger than the *edulis*, though that could just be a factor of a smaller industry with lower production. They are also about twice the price of the East Coast *edulises*, but are still absolutely worth it.

North American mussels are a tremendous success story: a brand-new, truly sustainable aquaculture business, started from scratch in the late '70s — though it took some convincing here in Canada and the United States.

Mussels on both coasts are largely grown in "suspension," hanging from ropes, sometimes attached to rafts. This keeps them away from predators, gives them more food, and makes them easier to harvest. There is some harvesting of wild, bottom-grown mussels, especially in Maine and Massachusetts, but it is not a major part of the industry.

Gnocchi with Mussels and Tomato Sauce

*Gnocchi is fairly easy to make at home in small batches, and I enjoy the simplicity
of this preparation. Both the pasta and the mussels can be made a day or two in advance.
This means you can throw it together quickly come dinnertime. I prefer using West Coast mussels, like
Saltspring Island, as they tend to be a bit bigger, but Atlantic mussels are fine, too. Italians will advise
against putting cheese on seafood pasta, but I figure whatever floats your boat.*

500 g (1 lb) Saltspring or Atlantic
  mussels

300 mL (1¼ cups) water

3 medium white potatoes

1 egg

425 mL (1¾ cups) all-purpose flour +
  another 325 mL (1⅓ cups) for
  rolling out pasta

100 mL (6 tbsp + 2 tsp) olive oil

1 medium onion, finely diced

1 L (4 cups) jarred or canned peeled
  San Marzano tomatoes

Salt and pepper, to taste

60 mL (¼ cup) picked fresh tarragon
  leaves

Pecorino-Romano cheese, for grating
  (optional)

Rinse the mussels under cold running water. Discard any that don't try to close or that have cracked shells. Using a paring knife or your fingers, remove beards (the little tufts of hair sticking out of the mussels) and discard.

In a medium pot with a lid, over high heat, bring water to a boil. Once boiling, toss in mussels and cover. Let steam, stirring once, for about 7 minutes. Mussels should be open and meats should be firm. Not all will have cooked, but that's okay (they'll have an opportunity to cook further in the sauce). Remove from heat, cool, and drain, saving the cooking liquid. Pull the meat from the shells and refrigerate, with reserved cooking liquid, in an airtight container for up to 5 days. Discard shells.

In a saucepan of salted water, boil potatoes (peel on) until tender. Rinse under cold running water until just cool enough to handle. Peel potatoes and transfer to a large bowl. Mash potatoes well. Stir in egg and flour, and mix until a soft dough forms. Shape it into a ball, cover tightly in plastic wrap, and set aside on the counter.

In a medium pot over low heat, heat oil. Add onion and sauté for about 10 minutes, until softened. Add tomatoes and reserved mussel cooking liquid, and cook, uncovered, for 30 to 45 minutes, until cooking liquid is reduced by about one-third. Season with salt and pepper, to taste. Set aside.

Fill a medium pot three-quarters full of water, and salt it generously. Place it on high heat. Cut off a 150 g (5 oz) chunk of dough (re-wrap the rest and set aside). On a large wooden cutting board, sprinkle a generous amount of flour. Using your hands, roll the dough into a ball. Place it on the floured cutting board and, using your palms, roll it into a long cylinder, about 1 cm (½ inch) in diameter. Cut the cylinder widthwise into 2-cm (¾-inch) chunks. Using the tines of a fork, make an impression on each piece (this will help the sauce stick to the gnocchi). Working in batches so as not to crowd the pot, drop pasta pieces into the boiling salted water and cook for about 8 minutes. Using a slotted spoon, remove the cooked gnocchi from the water, let drain, and put in a large bowl. Drizzle with some olive oil to keep them from sticking together. Repeat until all the dough is used.

Once all the gnocchi is cooked, ladle about 500 mL (2 cups) of the tomato sauce into a saucepan. Add half the cooked pasta, half the reserved mussels, and half the tarragon. Turn the heat to medium, and warm for about 4 minutes, just until heated through. Divide between two serving plates. Repeat with the remaining pasta, mussels, and tarragon. Add cheese, or don't.

Serves 2 as a main course

MUSSEL SOUP

There is a classic mussel soup recipe, "Billi Bi Soup," from the 1970s New York Times *cookbook by Craig Claiborne and Pierre Franey. It's a great recipe, and I recommend looking it up. It has a funny instruction in the middle of it, though: "Save just one mussel for each bowl, as garnish." Back in the '60s and '70s, the mussels that were available were strictly bottom-harvested, and tended to be fairly sandy and gritty. The juice was the important part, and needed to be strained. Happily, today I would recommend including as many mussels as you like.*

OCTOPUS

ORIGIN: *Worldwide*

AVAILABILITY: *Year-round*

COMMON FORMS: *Whole, frozen; tentacles, frozen; very occasionally whole, fresh*

STOCK STATUS: *Wildly variable; little information available, though most stocks seem reasonably healthy; avoid African and Asian/Southeast Asian product*

SOURCE: *All catch is wild*

ALTERNATIVES: *squid*

ALWAYS A POPULAR item in Asia and the Mediterranean region, octopus has started to find its way onto more and more menus in North America, especially in larger cities, as it provides a dramatic, Instagram-ready plate. It is also delicious. Octopus generally requires a long poaching period before a short time on the grill, although there are methods, such as hanging and air-drying, or beating on a rock 100 times, that can eliminate the poaching step.

Octopuses tend to live short lives, reproduce prolifically, and have for a long time been fished without any concern for their status. Now that they have been gaining in popularity, concern is growing about the long-term health of the population. There are a few types of octopus that we eat: common, red, day, night, giant Pacific, hubb, and a few others. Most of the fish caught on the West Coast of North America via pots and traps is considered to be sustainable, though there is little management actually in place. It's the same story in Spain, Portugal, and Greece: Pot and trap harvesting methods are good, as they create minimal bycatch and restrict the fishing effort, but other methods, such as trawling, have a more significant impact and are not considered good options. Octopus from Asian countries such as Vietnam, and North African nations like Mauritania and Morocco, are generally thought of as poorly managed, or not managed at all, with damaging harvest methods. In addition, much of the octopus used in North American sushi restaurants is often marked as a product of Japan, though it has almost inevitably been imported to Japan from places like Vietnam and Morocco, and been

relabelled, thus putting much of what we eat in doubt.

Due to their unique biology, there is potential for a long-term, healthy octopus fishery. But there needs to be more information available, and consumers will have to demand better-sourced products, if we wish to see this happen. For now, as long as you can find well-caught North American or European octopus, enjoy. But be aware that much of what is being served, especially in restaurants, is not likely coming from these fisheries.

Whole Baby Octopus with Tomatillo Salsa

Octopuses are very intelligent creatures, and it's certainly possible that they will one day rise up and take over the world. But until that day comes, this dish is pretty tasty. The combination of charred octopus and tomatillo gets me every time.

For the salsa:

300 mL (1¼ cups) tomatillos, halved

90 g (6 tbsp) minced white onion

45 g (3 tbsp) minced garlic

2 Anaheim chilies, seeded, ribbed, and minced

10 mL (2 tsp) ground cumin

15 g (0.5 oz) fresh thyme leaves

30 mL (2 tbsp) granulated sugar

20 mL (1 tbsp + 1 tsp) salt

50 g (1.8 oz) fresh coriander stems, finely chopped

75 mL (⅓ cup) white vinegar

100 mL (6 tbsp + 2 tsp) water

For the octopus:

400 to 500 g (14 to 16 oz) baby octopus, beak removed, rinsed

500 mL (2 cups) fish stock or court bouillon (see recipe page 225)

100 mL (6 tbsp + 2 tsp) grapeseed or other high-heat oil

Salt and pepper

1 lemon, halved

High-quality olive oil

Flat-leaf parsley leaves, roughly chopped, for garnish

To make the salsa: In a medium pot, on medium-low heat, combine tomatillos, onion, garlic, chilies, cumin, thyme, sugar, salt, coriander, and half each of the vinegar and water. Simmer for about 20 minutes. Remove from heat. Using a stand or immersion blender, purée (in batches, if needed), using a bit of the remaining water and vinegar to reach desired consistency (salsa should be soft and chunky, but not too watery).

To make the octopus: In a large pot, over medium-low heat, simmer octopus in stock or court bouillon for about an hour, until tender. Remove and drain, drying with paper towel as well as you can. Place octopus in a large bowl. Add grapeseed oil, salt, and pepper, and toss until well coated.

Get charcoal grill fairly hot (about 250°C/480°F). Grill octopus, turning every minute or two, for a total of 6 or 7 minutes, until the flesh takes on dark brown to black markings (the meat is already well cooked, so grilling is to add flavour and texture). Transfer grilled octopus to a bowl, and squeeze lemon overtop. Drizzle with a healthy amount of olive oil and toss in chopped parsley leaves.

Serve hot, alongside room-temperature salsa.

Serves 6 as an appetizer

OYSTERS

ORIGIN: *Worldwide*

AVAILABILITY: *Year-round*

COMMON FORMS: *Whole, live in-shell; shucked meat*

STOCK STATUS: *Very good, no concerns*

SOURCE: *Most of the harvest is cultivated to some degree; some wild product is available*

ALTERNATIVES: *clams, especially littleneck and topneck*

LOVE 'EM OR HATE 'EM, it seems very few people are ambivalent about oysters. Poorly shucked, not the freshest, prepared using bad advice . . . there are all kinds of ways an oyster can go wrong. Right off the bat, though, it has to be said that different regions produce vastly different oyster flavours and textures. If, for example, your first oyster was in Seattle, it would be a completely different eating experience than one from Nova Scotia.

If you'd like to enjoy oysters at home, the most important skill to obtain is learning how to shuck them properly.

I've read — and written — many words on the subject, most of which are not helpful. You really need to watch a video or talk to a shucker to truly master the technique. And practice is key.

You can purchase oysters a few days in advance, no problem. Typically, West Coast oysters will last up to 1 week in the fridge, and East Coast can easily last 2 weeks. Make sure you put them in a crisper drawer, away from drafts, and have a wet cloth above and below them. Keep them moist, but not in water or ice that will melt into water.

WEST COAST

Usually referred to as gigas (pronounced *jie-gas*), these oysters tend to be fleshy and a bit creamy, with notes of melon, avocado, and/or cucumber. Historically, they were also on the larger side, though that is finally changing with the popularity of "tumbled" oysters, such as Kusshi and Shigoku, or naturally smaller ones, like the Kumamoto. Other varieties that grow out West include the tiny Olympia, the Virginica (or East Coast style), and the flat (or European style). These account for just a tiny amount of the West Coast production, though.

✦

EAST COAST

Again, dominated by one main species, the Virginica, East Coast oysters can range from quite small and delicate (usually northern regions, like Prince Edward Island or New Brunswick) to big and meaty (Long Island Sound and southward). They generally have a milder flavour with a sweeter finish and a less complex saltiness.

✦

EUROPE

Two varieties are commonly seen, the *edulis* (also called the "flat" or "native") and the gigas. The flats are known for their distinct copper and citrus flavours and very dense meat; whereas the gigas are more tender and briny, with that melon/cucumber flavour. They tend to be less creamy than their North American counterparts.

Oysters with Leeks and Bacon

Different oysters have different flavours. Recipes that work well with an East Coast oyster might not match up with a West Coast oyster. This recipe is intended to be paired with a meaty Atlantic oyster — subtle and silky.

12 large East Coast oysters, rinsed

22 mL (1½ tbsp) butter

1 large or 2 small leeks, finely minced

100 g (3.5 oz) slab double-smoked bacon, cut into small cubes

45 mL (3 tbsp) dry white wine

45 mL (3 tbsp) beef stock

45 mL (3 tbsp) heavy or whipping (35%) cream

15 g (0.5 oz) finely chopped fresh thyme leaves (1 or 2 sprigs, picked)

Preheat oven to 200°C (400°F).

Over a bowl (to collect "liquor" or juice), shuck oysters and set aside. Wash the rounded halves of the shells and arrange, shucked-side up, in a single layer on a baking sheet. Place in preheated oven, to warm.

In a skillet, over medium heat, melt butter. Add leeks and bacon, and cook for about 8 minutes, until onion is softened but not browned and bacon is cooked through. Add wine and beef stock, and increase heat to high. Cook, stirring occasionally, until liquid is reduced by half. Stir in cream. Cook for about 3 minutes, until sauce has thickened. Add the oyster meat and thyme, and remove from heat.

Remove pan from oven, and spoon an oyster and some of the cream mixture into each shell. Return to oven and heat for an additional 6 to 10 minutes, depending on the size of your oysters. You want the edges of the oyster to "frill" up, and the sauce to bubble in the shells. Remove the pan from the oven, and serve hot.

Serves 2 as an appetizer

Fermented Hot Sauce

I only serve a couple of condiments with my oysters: a homemade fermented pepper hot sauce and a simple mignonette (see next page). To get the hot sauce right, you'll need about a month (or more, if you like), but it's worth the wait. I like the mellower flavour fermenting provides.

2 L (8 cups) warm water

120 mL (8 tbsp) kosher salt

4 × 1 L (4 cup) Mason jars, sterilized

12 cloves garlic

3 L (12 cups) hot red peppers (I use cayenne or Anaheim peppers, nothing too crazy), stems removed

Fine cheesecloth

In a large bowl, combine warm water and salt (to make a brine), and stir until salt has completely dissolved.

Put 3 cloves of garlic in each Mason jar. Pack as many peppers as will comfortably fit into each jar — if the peppers crack a bit, that's okay.

Pour prepared brine into each jar of peppers, leaving about 2.5 cm (1 inch) headspace. The peppers should be completely submerged, and they need to be kept submerged during the fermenting process, so weigh them down with a smaller lid or a ramekin. Cover each jar with some fine cheesecloth, and affix with a rubber band. Leave in a cool, dark place for at least a month — up to a year — checking occasionally. If you see a bit of white mold developing, just scrape it off.

When the peppers are ready, transfer them (reserve the brine) to a food processor. Process on low speed, gradually adding a bit of brine until you reach a texture you like. I usually keep the seeds in my sauce, but you can run it through a food mill to remove them, if you want.

Pour the sauce into clean jars and seal. It will keep in the fridge for a year.

Makes 4 L (16 cups) hot sauce

— Simple Mignonette —

We all have our philosophy on something as simple as mignonette — no one is right or wrong. Mine has apple cider vinegar and white wine because they are products that come from the same regions as oysters do. I'm not a fan of red wine in my mignonette, as I wouldn't recommend drinking too much red wine with oysters.

200 mL (¾ cup + 5 tsp) apple cider vinegar

1 large or 2 small shallots, minced

15 mL (1 tbsp) cracked black pepper

200 mL (¾ cup + 5 tsp) Riesling or other fresh white wine

In a bowl, combine vinegar, shallots, and pepper. Set aside to marinate for 10 to 15 minutes. Stir in wine.

Mignonette will keep in an airtight container in the refrigerator for a few days. Discard when shallots get soft. Best made same day as eating.

Makes 400 mL (1⅔ cups; enough for up to 100 oysters)

I'm not a fan of red wine in my mignonette, as I wouldn't recommend drinking too much red wine with oysters.

THE DIFFERENCE BETWEEN GROWING AND FISHING OYSTERS

Most oysters that we see now are cultivated or farmed, but pockets of vibrant wild fishing still occur. Prince Edward Island has one of them. About half of the Island's oyster production comes from the wild fishery, which has remained fairly stable over the past 30 years (it may have even increased). In general, oysters are "tonged" from the bottom of rivers and bays. They grow in depths of up to 6 metres (20 feet), though most are at 1.5 to 3 metres (5 to 10 feet). The fishers will typically wait for low tide, as their tongs — essentially two rakes hinged together — tend to max out at 2.5 metres (8 feet) long, though some will wield "rakes" up to almost 4 metres (12 feet) in length, which can be very hard to manage on a windy day.

These oysters are then taken to a buyer and graded for quality, and the fishers get paid according to the grade. Buyers will then put the oysters back in the water, on their "lease" (acreage in the ocean) for a minimum of two weeks to ensure they are

Opposite: Legendary oyster fisher and farmer George Dowdle, from New London, P.E.I.
Above: A fisher harvesting oysters from the wild fishery on P.E.I.

"depurated" (clear of any bacteria). This depuration stage helps to reduce the risk of illness significantly, as it's difficult for buyers to know how long the oysters were out of the water, unrefrigerated, between fishing and buying. There is also a chance that higher-than-normal levels of bacteria exist in the spot the oysters were harvested from.

Harvesting of wild oysters is difficult and highly seasonal work. A very good fisher might take in about $15,000 a year, and they will usually supplement this with income from another source. There will always be a wild fishery, but the main limits on it are human, not environmental.

When you want to stock your oyster farm, you have a couple of options: spreading baby oysters loose on the bottom of your lease or acreage, or putting babies into floating bags. Once the bags have the appropriate volume of oysters, they are

> *Harvesting of wild oysters is difficult and highly seasonal work.*

strung along the surface of the lease. The bags get flipped regularly to keep them clean. Being higher up in the water column, the oysters get more food, have a longer growing season, and are less susceptible to predators. Other than that, there is no difference

between a wild and a cultivated oyster: They both are given all-natural food — no additives — and lots of care and attention. Up North, it takes 3 to 5 years to get an oyster to market; whereas further South, like Alabama, you need only a year or less. It's all a function of water temperature, not genetics or hormones.

As with the wild fishery, cultivating oysters is hard work, but it can be done year-round, and the grower obviously has more control over the quality, harvest schedule, and scale. The cultivated side of oysters has been key to keeping up with the tremendous increase in demand over the last 20 years.

Opposite: Word gets out fast when you're on a "pile." Some spots are prolific year after year, while some need a few years to recover.
Above: Thumbnail-sized oysters in a floating oyster grading shed, Cascumpec Bay, P.E.I.
Overleaf: Oyster bags on a lease, Savage Harbour, P.E.I.

Above: A floating oyster-grading shed.
Below: Martin O'Brien, oyster grower, Cascumpec Bay Oyster Company.

John tags along on an oyster boat on Casumpec Bay.

—PERIWINKLES—

ORIGIN: *North Atlantic*
AVAILABILITY: *Year-round, though largely spring and summer*
COMMON FORMS: *Whole, live in-shell*
STOCK STATUS: *Good, little concern*
SOURCE: *All catch is wild*
ALTERNATIVES: *whelks, clams*

PEOPLE OFTEN CONFUSE land snails and sea snails. Both types are gastropods, and there are thousands of varieties of each. Of the edible sea snails, some of them, such as conch, grow to be much larger than the common land snails served stuffed with garlic and herbs in French restaurants. Others, like periwinkles, are quite small — barely the size of a nickel. Most sea snails have ornate, fluted shells that can sometimes be brightly coloured. The periwinkle is much humbler, with a smooth brownish shell slightly tinted the most beautiful shade of blue.

Periwinkles live on rocks, sometimes under water, sometimes just splashed by the waves, and are picked by hand. They typically are not sandy, so they only require a quick rinse under cold running water before you give them a quick steam/boil to get them to "pop" out of their shells. Pick the meat out with an opened paper-clip or toothpick, and dunk it in a mixture of white vinegar and butter. Or get ambitious and incorporate them into a sauce, as a Northern crawfish type of vibe. Don't save the steaming broth, as it will not be delicious (unlike broth made from clams and mussels).

Make sure to cook periwinkles in small batches. That way, if you happen to get a bad one — you'll know because it will stink somewhat like ammonia — you can just discard that batch, instead of dumping the whole lot of them. Periwinkles have an amazing, rich flavour, full of seaweed and iodine, and are certainly worth the effort of the plucking.

SCALLOPS

ORIGIN: *Worldwide*

AVAILABILITY: *Year-round, though each species has its own season; be aware that there is potential for mislabelling, intentionally or unintentionally, due to the nature of the shellfish; care must be taken to ensure you are getting what you pay for*

COMMON FORMS: *Shucked meat, raw, fresh, or frozen; occasionally, live in-shell*

STOCK STATUS: *Healthy, low concern, especially in North America*

SOURCE: *Almost all catch is wild; very small amount of smaller cultivated scallops*

ALTERNATIVES: *razor clams, monkfish*

IF GEODUCKS ARE the king of shellfish, then scallops have to be the queen. Sweet and addictive, equally delicious raw or cooked, scallops have taken a prominent place on many menus, and justifiably so. Most scallops (99 percent) are harvested by dragging the ocean floor, which sounds terrible, but is generally harmless, when the scale of the damage is taken into consideration. Yes, the technique is harmful to the bottom, but the dragnets tend to take very little bycatch, and the actual amount of floor disturbed is tiny, relative to the total size of the sea bottom targeted. Harvests have been pretty steady over the past 15 years, indicating a reasonably healthy fishery. A tiny amount of "diver-caught" scallops are in the market, but they are a minute fraction of the actual harvest. If your local seafood restaurant/store claims to have diver-caught scallops, I would question the owner to be sure they understand what they are saying. It's certainly possible, just not very likely. Scallops are unique among bivalve shellfish (oysters, clams, mussels, etc.), in that they are generally sold out of the shell, pre-shucked (processed), and most of the actual creature is removed. In fact, what most people think of as a scallop is, in fact, just the muscle that opens and closes their shells. It represents only about 10 percent of the actual animal's weight; the rest is discarded at sea. There is a historical reason for this that has to do with paralysis.

Scallops fished from certain areas will cause paralytic shellfish poisoning (PSP) when eaten whole. (Interestingly, when eaten alone, the adductor muscle does not cause this reaction.) Thus, the historical tradition of shucking the scallop for only the muscle meat began. Certain scallops (for example, bay scallops) fished from specific areas can safely be eaten whole, and it's safe to assume your seafood provider will make sure that you are being served something harmless. Any scallop that has the potential to carry PSP toxin will be shucked long before it gets to you.

HOW TO SHUCK A SCALLOP

Shucking scallops is pretty easy: Rinse them quickly under cold running water and, using a sharp paring knife, run the blade along the top shell of each scallop. Try to stay as close to the shell as possible, to save the scallop meat. Remove the top shell. You will be looking at a large white "scallop," surrounded by a bunch of brownish stuff, and a black belly at the back end of the shell. Put your knife under that black part, and your thumb on top of it, and pull upward. Most of the goopy things will lift right off. Keep pulling, until you have separation. If you need to scrape a few more things away, no problem. You want to be left with just the white part of the scallop, the adductor mussel. Some people also save, and eat, the bright pink/orange gonad of the scallop, but that's up to you. Give the scallop (still attached to the shell) another quick rinse to get rid of any last bits, and slice it off the shell, again trying your best to preserve the meat.

LIVE SCALLOP CEVICHE

Firm, with rich flavours, scallops can stand up to a lot of treatments, but sometimes I just want to let the fish speak for itself.

6 live scallops, shucked from the shell and cleaned (see page 80)

1 medium white onion, finely diced

300 mL (1¼ cups) fresh lime juice

1 Anaheim or cayenne chili pepper, seeded and minced

½ bunch fresh coriander, stems and leaves separated, roughly chopped

Juice from 1 grapefruit

45 mL (3 tbsp) cane sugar

1 grapefruit, peeled and cut into small chunks

High-quality olive oil

Finishing salt (light flakes, not iodized)

In a non-reactive bowl, combine scallops, onion, and lime juice. Cover and refrigerate for about 3 hours.

Transfer marinated scallops to a cutting board. To the onion and lime juice mixture, add chili, coriander stems, grapefruit juice, and sugar. Set aside.

Using a sharp knife, cut each scallop horizontally into 4 equal rounds or "coins." Fan each sliced scallop over a small serving plate. Spoon chili mixture overtop and around the scallop. Garnish with grapefruit pieces and coriander leaves. Drizzle with olive oil, and dust with finishing salt.

Serves 4 to 6 as an appetizer

Sea Urchin

ORIGIN: *Worldwide*

AVAILABILITY: *Year-round*

COMMON FORMS: *Whole, live in-shell; fresh shucked gonad meat*

STOCK STATUS: *Good, little concern*

SOURCE: *All catch is wild*

ALTERNATIVES: *none, really; perhaps scallop roe*

UNTIL FAIRLY RECENTLY, sea urchin was something that was completely ignored in North America, outside of Asian (mostly sushi) restaurants. Whether referred to as "uni" or "urchin," we are talking about the gonads (reproductive organs) of the creature. This is the only part that gets eaten. Urchin shells are spiny, strange-looking things that need to be cracked open or cut into with scissors to extract the golden-orange innards.

When very fresh, urchin has a rich seaweed and cucumber flavour, almost sweet. Urchin oxidizes quickly, and low-quality or older meat will have a heavy, musky smell and flavour. Some seafood has a longer-than-expected shelf life — urchin is not one of them. Traditionally served atop rice or simply plated, the flavour of the urchin is generally allowed to stand on its own, as it needs no enhancing. Newer interpretations can include creamed urchin or making it part of a crudo/ceviche, such as scallop. The flavours of these two tend to play well off each other.

Urchin is found worldwide, in both the Atlantic and Pacific oceans. It is harvested by diving almost exclusively, and is a well-managed fishery. Urchin will pick up very different flavours, depending on its source. California urchin will taste markedly different than Maine urchin or Danish urchin. It's hard to say that one is better than the other; it really just boils down to personal taste. And, truthfully, more important than where it comes from is how it has been handled and how fresh it is. I have had a lot of truly terrible urchin, even in extremely

high-end restaurants, and it's my belief that many chefs, and most average diners, really haven't had great, truly fresh urchin. If they had, they would reject these substandard products out of hand. For this reason, sadly, I rarely order it in restaurants anymore. I'll happily collect a few and crack them open, but I'd rather keep the memory of those moments alive than try to chase it by playing urchin roulette at some random restaurant. Buyer beware!

—SHRIMP—

ORIGIN: *Worldwide*

AVAILABILITY: *Year-round, though not all species*

COMMON FORMS: *Heads removed; occasionally whole,
even more rarely live; frozen, shell on and off*

STOCK STATUS: *Wildly variable; in general,
North American shrimp are the best choice*

SOURCE: *Most larger shrimp are farmed, though
U.S. Gulf shrimp are wild; smaller shrimp tend to be wild*

ALTERNATIVES: *langoustine, crawfish*

THE INTERNATIONAL LABOUR Organization (ILO) is an agency of the United Nations that investigates worker complaints. Along with several news agencies, the ILO is currently trying to pressure several Southeast Asian nations into reforming the conditions in their fishing industries. In March 2017, a report from the investigating committee noted that the majority of fishers do not have any form of written contract of their employment, and where contracts do exist, it is alleged that signatures were obtained under duress. Additional allegations include 20-hour workdays, a complete lack of medical care, non-payment of wages, forced abduction of workers, and physical abuse of fishers, up to and including murder. These problems are especially prominent in the shrimp industry. North America imports over 90 percent of its shrimp, mostly from Southeast Asia. If you have ever eaten a shrimp, it is almost inevitable that you have eaten the product of slave labour.

This doesn't mean, however, that you should stop eating shrimp altogether. It just means that it's worth paying attention to the source of the shrimp at your local seafood counter. There are many good to great choices available. Some of these include wild British Columbia (B.C.) and Washington spot prawns, B.C. side stripe shrimp, U.S. Gulf shrimp, Quebec Matane shrimp, Argentine red shrimp, Northern or Arctic shrimp, and containment-farmed shrimp from Ontario, Minnesota, Indiana, and Massachusetts.

Shrimp is the number one seafood eaten in North America, and it has historically been a pretty inexpensive product. We now know that low price is simply not sustainable if we want shrimp that are correctly farmed and humanely caught. I hesitate to put numbers on fish prices, because they can be so variable, but high-quality wild shrimp will typically cost at least $10 per pound in the shop, and farmed shrimp $15 per pound, though prices for high-demand, short-season shrimp, such as spot prawns, can go as high as $30 per pound. No one likes to pay more than they are used to for a common product, but in the case of shrimp, it's become necessary. On the upside, these good shrimp choices tend to be much tastier than traditional shrimp, and support a healthy, well-paying fishery. It's totally worth it.

HOW TO CLEAN A SHRIMP

To clean shrimp, use a very sharp paring knife to cut lengthwise down the back of the shell from the head to the tail, penetrating about a third of the way into the flesh. The exposed membrane may or may not contain dark matter, which is a form of intestine. Using the tip of the knife, simply pluck it out and wipe it away on a cloth or paper towel. Rinse the shrimp under cool running water.

— NORTHERN SHRIMP ROLLS —

*There used to be a nice shrimp fishery in Maine, though it's been mostly closed
the past couple of years. Happily, there are still shrimp in the Saint Lawrence River (Matane
shrimp), and off the coast of Newfoundland (Arctic shrimp). All these smaller, cold-water shrimp
have a beautiful flavour and a softer texture, but it does take a lot of them to fill a person.
This variation on a lobster roll aims to fix that problem.*

2 egg yolks

15 mL (1 tbsp) Dijon mustard

5 mL (1 tsp) salt

200 mL (¾ cup + 5 tsp) vegetable oil

Juice from 1 lemon

1 bunch of fresh dill, fronds only,
finely chopped

Freshly cracked black pepper, to taste

400 g (14 oz) shrimp, cooked, peeled,
deveined, and chilled

4 small top-split buns (if you can
manage it)

75 mL (⅓ cup) butter, for frying

To make the mayonnaise: In a bowl, whisk together egg yolks, mustard, and salt for about a minute. Start adding oil, very slowly, while whisking continuously, until the mixture has emulsified and you have a creamy-looking blend. If it's a bit thick, whisk in a bit more oil, until you reach your desired consistency. Add lemon juice and dill, and stir to combine. Season with pepper, to your taste. Add shrimp to dill mayonnaise, and stir gently.

Split the top of your buns. In a skillet over medium-high heat, melt butter. Spread the buns apart at the tops and toast, split-side down, just until lightly golden. Fill each bun equally with the shrimp mixture.

Of course, fries are a common side for this kind of sandwich, but I'm more likely to serve it with a simple green or tomato salad.

Makes 4 nice sandwiches or 6 slender ones

HEAD-ON SHRIMP IN GARLIC BUTTER

Okay, I know . . . shrimp in garlic butter. But I'm telling you, when you can find truly fresh, never frozen, head-on shrimp, this is all you want to do with them. The thing is, it's getting harder and harder to find shrimp this way. First, they must be from North America, which is already tricky, and then you need to find them live, or at the very least fresh, which limits your chances even more. But it's worth the search. Best bets in North America are in Washington State and British Columbia, when the spot prawns are running; down in Apalachicola, if you can meet up with a packer there; or in Ontario, where there are currently two active shrimp farms. I'm sure there are others. When you cook the shrimp, it has to be shell-on. Never mind all that jazz about "cleaning" them. The shells help to keep the flesh moist, and the heads have all kinds of sweet fat inside, which is fun to suck out when you twist them off the rest of the shrimp.

3 cloves garlic, minced

250 mL (1 cup) butter

12 nice head-on fresh shrimp

Zest and juice of 1 lemon

½ bunch fresh flat-leaf parsley, leaves only, roughly chopped

Salt and pepper, to taste

In a medium sauté pan, over medium heat, combine garlic and butter. Just as it all starts bubbling, add shrimp, making sure they are all evenly distributed and touching the pan. Cook for about 2 minutes, and then flip. Cook other side for 2 to 3 minutes. Transfer the shrimp to a serving plate, reserving pan, and set shrimp aside.

To the pan, over high heat, stir in lemon zest and juice. The butter and juices will start to brown. When the butter has reduced by about one-third and just begun to thicken, remove the pan from heat. Pour the garlic butter over the shrimp. Garnish with chopped parsley leaves, add a bit of salt and pepper, and serve.

Serves 2 as an appetizer or 1 as a main course

OKONOMIYAKI

Hiroshima and Osaka both lay claim to being the originators of this dish yet have very different styles. The version I'm including is closer to the Osaka style. Either way, this cabbage and Nagaimo yam pancake is addictive.

For the dashi (stock):

250 mL (1 cup) water

25 g or ¼ of a standard 100 g package (10 tbsp) katsuobushi flakes

For the pancake:

325 mL (1⅓ cups) all-purpose flour

250 mL (1 cup) dashi

2 medium eggs

150 g (5 oz) Nagaimo yam, peeled and grated (it will be slimy and very wet)

300 g (10 oz) finely shredded cabbage

100 g (3.5 oz) peeled and chopped shrimp

30 mL (2 tbsp) vegetable oil

4 strips bacon

Kewpie mayonnaise

Okonomi sauce

Katsuobushi flakes, for garnish

Green onion, finely chopped (for garnish)

To make the dashi: In a saucepan, bring water and katsuobushi to a boil. Remove from heat, and let steep for 20 minutes. Strain through a fine-mesh sieve (discard solids) and set aside. Will keep in an airtight container in the refrigerator for up to 10 days.

To make the pancake: In a bowl, whisk together flour, dashi, eggs, and yam until smooth. Stir in cabbage and shrimp.

In a 25-cm (10-inch) skillet, over medium heat, heat oil. Lay bacon strips alongside each other, creating a base for the pancake. Pour cabbage mixture onto the bacon, flattening it out to cover the bacon evenly. Cover and cook, undisturbed, for 8 minutes. Uncover and flip carefully. Cover and cook for an additional 8 to 10 minutes.

Flip pancake once more, and slide onto a serving plate. Drizzle with mayo and okonomi sauce, and sprinkle with katsuobushi and green onion.

Serve immediately, while the katsuobushi flakes are still moving.

Makes 3 pancakes. Serves 3 as a main course or 4 to 6 as an appetizer.

SQUID

ORIGIN: *Worldwide*
AVAILABILITY: *Year-round, though largely spring and summer*
COMMON FORMS: *frozen, cleaned and gutted; fresh, whole*
STOCK STATUS: *Overall good, little concern*
SOURCE: *All catch is wild*
ALTERNATIVES: *surf clams, cuttlefish*

"As much as we know about squid, we still don't know that much."

— Bruce Robison, Ph.D., Monterey Bay Aquarium Research Institute

SINCE THE 1980s, calamari has been an unkillable part of many menus. And, to many in the fishing industry, squid seems to be an unkillable fishery. Billions of pounds are harvested annually around the world — in South America alone, over 2 billion pounds a year is not unheard of — yet our knowledge of the squid's biomass and of the health of the stocks is basically zero. It's essentially an uncountable fish (cephalopod, if we're being technical).

Most of the concerns raised by rating agencies focus on harvest methods rather than quantities. In general, squid from India, China, and Southeast Asia is not well regarded, due to the use of destructive fishing gear (otter, or bottom, trawls). Most of the North and South American squid, especially market and Humboldt squid from the West Coast, is caught by jigging, seining, or midwater trawl, and is rated as "least concern." In other words, fill your boots and eat all you'd like. Squid reproduce prolifically and, for the most part, live less than 2 years. They are carnivorous, voracious, and provide food for a lot of sea creatures, as well.

Fairly easy to clean, squid contain a dramatic black ink that can be used to colour bread and pasta. Mostly, folks eat squid fried in "tube and tentacle" form. The tentacle is pretty obvious, but the tube actually comes from slicing the head in a particular way. Amazingly, some people are too squeamish to eat the tentacles, so some restaurants actually offer "tube only" squid.

HOW TO CLEAN A SQUID

The first step in cleaning a squid is to remove the "backbone" and beak. They are the hard bits and are easy enough to get rid of. Just pull the beak (it is whitish in colour) from underneath the tentacles. Then reach inside the tube of the squid and pull out the backbone (it is clear and almost looks like plastic); usually it slides out in one piece. You'll also notice a small sac that contains the squid ink — remove this. Then remove the darker skin on the outside of the squid: Using a paring knife, scrape at the skin until you can grab it, and then pull it off (it should lift off reasonably easily with a firm tug). Cut off the "wings" (the flaps on either side of the tube). After a good rinse under cold running water, the squid is now ready to be cooked.

HOW TO MAKE SQUID-INK BREAD

To make beautiful squid-ink bread that has a slightly different flavour, use about 10 mL (2 tsp) of ink for every 1 kg (2 lb) of dough. Knead it in at the very end. The ink is non-toxic and won't change the bread too much, but it will be a standout change of pace.

SIMPLE GRILLED SQUID

Most commonly, the squid you buy at the shop will be cleaned for you.
It may be "whole, cleaned," which has both the body and the tentacles, or it may be just
the "tubes" or bodies. Nothing much needs to be done to prepare cleaned squid, except for a
thorough rinse under cold running water, checking for any hard bits that might be left behind,
and then patting dry with paper towel. If you buy truly whole squid,
it will need to be cleaned (see page 94).

10 pieces whole squid, cleaned, tubes
and tentacles separated
50 mL (3 tbsp + 1 tsp) grapeseed or
other high-heat oil
Zest and juice of 2 lemons
1 bunch fresh flat-leaf parsley,
leaves only, chopped
Salt and pepper, to taste
The best olive oil you've got

You'll need a hot charcoal grill for this. Gas may get you there, but I doubt it. Most gas grills don't generate enough heat. The trick is to cook the squid as quickly as possible, so as not to toughen it up.

Separate the tubes from the tentacles. Dry outer parts of the squid as thoroughly as possible. This is important — the dryer, the better. Rub the squid all over with oil, and toss onto the hot grill. Cook for about 2 minutes per side.

Transfer the cooked squid to a medium bowl. Working quickly, toss with lemon zest and juice, parsley, and salt and pepper.

Plate everything, and drizzle with a healthy amount of olive oil. Hopefully, if you dried the squid enough, and your coals were very hot, you will have a nice char on your squid, as well as having a delicious plate of food.

Serves 4 to 6 as an appetizer

TIP

This recipe really only works if you are using truly fresh squid. Squid that has been defrosted is good for many things, particularly frying, but the flavour and texture will have changed enough that the simplicity we're striving for here is lost.

WHELKS

ORIGIN: *Worldwide*
AVAILABILITY: *Year-round, though largely spring and summer*
COMMON FORMS: *Whole; shucked meat, jarred*
STOCK STATUS: *Overall good, little concern*
SOURCE: *All catch is wild*
ALTERNATIVES: *conch, clams, mussels*

TASTY LITTLE CARNIVORES, whelks have mostly fallen off the map in North America. Sometimes confused with conch (which are larger and herbivorous), the whelk has been fished so sporadically that we are not even sure of its "sustainable" level of harvest. Needless to say, the catch is quite small overall, and you shouldn't feel any guilt about eating these. Found primarily along the Eastern Seaboard, from Cape Breton to Florida, whelks are fished with traps similar to those used in lobster harvesting. The traps are baited and checked every couple of days. The method is very gentle on the environment, and selective in what it catches.

HOW TO PREPARE WHELK MEAT

Bring a large pot filled with well-salted water to a boil. Toss the live whelks in, cover, and cook for 8 to 10 minutes. Drain the whelks, and rinse under cold running water. Using a fork, gently pull the soft creatures out of their shells. Trim off the dark-coloured bits, which are about one-third of its body. All of the lighter-coloured parts are edible and tasty, reminiscent of scallop or clam meat. Alternatively, jarred or frozen whelks are also fantastic.

WHELKS IN SHERRY CREAM ON TOAST

A popular item at Honest Weight, chopped whelks slightly resemble cooked mushrooms, and they both pair well with Fino sherry. This recipe is a quick and easy crowd pleaser.

40 mL (2½ tbsp) olive oil

40 g (1.4 oz) shallots, finely minced

5 cloves garlic, finely minced

200 g (7 oz) shiitake mushrooms, roughly chopped

100 mL (6 tbsp + 2 tsp) Fino sherry

50 mL (3 tbsp + 1 tsp) heavy or whipping (35%) cream

200 g (7 oz) whelks, trimmed (see previous page) and roughly chopped

4 slices rye toast, crusts removed

30 g (1 oz) fresh chives, minced

In a skillet over low heat, combine oil, shallots, and garlic and cook for about 10 minutes, until shallots and garlic are softened but not browned. Add mushrooms and sherry, and increase heat to medium. Cook, stirring occasionally, until liquid is reduced by half, about 5 minutes. Stir in cream and whelks, and cook for another 5 minutes or so, just until everything is heated through. Remove pan from heat, and spoon mixture onto rye toasts, evenly. Garnish with chives.

Serves 6 to 8 as a snack or 4 as an appetizer

SMALL FISH

A good rule of thumb: the smaller the ocean creature, the better it is for you and the ocean.

Smelts, mackerel, perch, and the like, reproduce quickly, are plentiful, and can be fished using methods that have a minimal negative impact on the ocean environment. In addition, smaller fish are typically younger, and less likely to accumulate toxins and heavy metals, if that is a concern of yours. It's true that the tinier fish bring you in closer contact to bones, as there is a higher bone-to-meat ratio, but when cooked properly, the meat lifts very easily off the bone. Cooking the whole fish also improves the flavour and texture of the meat, as it keeps the flesh moist, and allows some of the fat and collagen to melt into the meat. Small fish really are some of the most guilt-free options in the sea.

Many small fish get a bad rap for not seeming as "fresh" as some of their larger brethren. A lot of this has to do with the lower value that we have placed on them. As different species of fish gain acceptance, they are handled better, and this results in a superior product by the time it reaches the fish counter. We need to celebrate these fish now, and eventually the distribution chain will respond.

For advice on handling and storage, see page 277.

HERRING

ORIGIN: *North Atlantic, Eastern Pacific (North and South America)*
AVAILABILITY: *Year-round, though largely spring and summer*
COMMON FORMS: *Whole, fresh; pickled; oiled; canned; smoked*
STOCK STATUS: *Overall good, little concern*
SOURCE: *All catch is wild*
ALTERNATIVES: *smelts, whiting*

FRESH, PICKLED, OILED, canned, smoked: Herring has sustained us in so many ways over the years. But herring is not just important to us; it's important to the ocean's ecology as well. A forage fish, herring are the ocean's biggest converter of zooplankton into energy. This means they eat plankton, which they store as energy, and in turn the herring are eaten by many other species of fish and birds. This natural process is crucial to the health of the world. And herring are revered the world over. Sort of.

North America has never really caught on, outside of small pockets. Certainly in the cod fishery, herring was an important bait fish, either fresh or lightly salted, until nets replaced handlining as the dominant fishing method in the 1970s. And a large amount of herring was smoked and shipped to Europe. Export markets continue to provide the bulk of the customers for the North American herring fishery. And bait continues to be the primary use for herring in Canada. Apparently the sea lions out West still enjoy a meal of herring, and will even swarm the boats when the nets are set!

Smoked herring has gone by a lot of names: kippers, bloaters, buckling, red herring. I love them all. In fact, we briefly considered calling Honest Weight "Buckling" until I was talked out of it. Apparently, it's still too obscure here, unlike in Europe. In fact, Scheveningen, a port town in the Netherlands, celebrates the first "green herring" of the season, when the fat content reaches 16 percent and the fish is at its sweetest. Even outside of festivals, herring carts are a common sight on streets, serving various pickled and smoked herring dishes.

Hopefully, the herring ship hasn't sailed on North American taste buds just yet.

LIONFISH

ORIGIN: *Southeastern Atlantic, Gulf of Mexico*
AVAILABILITY: *Year-round*
COMMON FORMS: *Fillets, fresh and frozen*
STOCK STATUS: *Excellent, an overabundance*
SOURCE: *All catch is wild*
ALTERNATIVES: *rockfish, snapper*

THE MOST DANGEROUS fish that you've probably never heard of, these natives of the Indo-Pacific were mostly seen only in North American aquariums until sometime in the '80s or '90s, when a few lionfish were released (or escaped) on the east coast of Florida. Typically, a random introduction like this wouldn't be cause for alarm, since the fish would have died in their new environs — or been eaten. Unfortunately, the lionfish proved to be a voracious and determined predator. They are highly successful hunters and resist being eaten themselves, thanks to eighteen venomous spines scattered around their body. You literally can't be too careful with the spines, as they will hurt worse than a bee sting. Lionfish are becoming a huge problem from Cape Hatteras down to the Caribbean.

Happily, they are also delicious! About the size of a rockfish (750 g to 1 kg/1½ to 2 lb) and easy to fillet — once you have the technique (maybe let your fishmonger take care of this) — lionfish yield meat that is pure white, mild to sweet, and holds up to many preparations, including ceviche. Sadly, they resist easy catching: Neither net nor handline work. Only spearing by divers has proven effective, which is very sustainable but also fairly expensive, raising the retail price. For the long-term health of the Southwest Atlantic habitats, the lionfish requires intensive control efforts. A culinary solution would be a big part of this control. We just need to teach chefs how to handle them, and somehow get consumers on board despite the premium price.

How Old Is That Fish Anyway?

Although some of us like to think that we live in a magical world where everything has been "caught yesterday" or "flown in daily," it's sadly not the case. If you happen to live in a coastal, food-obsessed city such as New York, Vancouver, or Los Angeles, or know some fishers, you can get some fish the same day (or the next), but for the vast majority of us, it's just not possible. At Honest Weight, in landlocked Toronto, you can see a chinook salmon caught off the coast of British Columbia on a Wednesday morning at the shop on Thursday afternoon because of good relationships with some committed suppliers like Organic Ocean. But this is not the typical experience.

Farmed fish certainly have a more predictable schedule than wild fish. Having worked on oyster and salmon farms, I know it's possible to harvest in New Brunswick on a Monday, ship to Boston on a Tuesday, and have it on a dining table on a Wednesday evening. Wild fish, however, have a different timeline. Some boats will head out for a few days, landing fish and keeping them well iced in their holds before returning to shore, meaning that some of the fish from that catch are already 3 days old. Add in packing and shipping times, and then reshipping when at the destination, and it's fairly common to be starting with a 5-day-old fish at a restaurant that says it "just landed." Of course, shipments of that fish into that particular city might only occur once a week. So even if the restaurant orders just enough for that evening and are always "just landing" that fish, it's from the same inventory. A lot of fish that landed at the distributor on Thursday at 4 days old will still be sold on the Monday at 8 days old, or even older. My guess is that the average age of a fillet, served in a non-coastal city, is 6 to 10 days old. And you know what? That's totally fine. It doesn't mean that the fish we are eating are "not fresh" or "bad." It just means that we have to recalibrate what we mean by "fresh."

Honestly, it's not always about how long ago it was caught. It's often more important to understand how it's been treated since. Fillets will degrade faster than whole fish. Ungutted whole fish will go soft faster than cleaned fish. Cold chain maintenance is more important than any of those things. There are lots of factors that contribute to fresh fish.

My guess is that the average age of a fillet, served in a non-coastal city, is 6 to 10 days old. And you know what? That's totally fine.

Instead of asking meaningless questions like "When did that come in?" — which put the person behind the counter on the defensive — use your senses: Does the fish look shiny or dull? If it's filleted, are there gaps in the flesh? If so, pass on it. Or ask to smell it. It should have a pleasant odour. I long for the day when servers in restaurants and folks behind fish counters don't have to gingerly dance around questions about the age of their fish. If you're in the store, judge for yourself. If you're in a restaurant, trust them. And if it tastes off, tell them. Don't be shy. Be an informed consumer.

MACKEREL

ORIGIN: *Worldwide*

AVAILABILITY: *Year-round*

COMMON FORMS: *Whole*

STOCK STATUS: *Good from North America; recently recovered in Europe; unknown elsewhere*

SOURCE: *All catch is wild*

ALTERNATIVES: *sardines, bonito*

OFTEN OVERLOOKED DUE to its perceived fishy taste, mackerel is a fantastic and flexible fish. Essentially a small tuna, it is very flavourful, though it does need to be fresh, as the high oil content in the flesh will cause it to spoil more quickly than less oily whitefish such as cod and halibut. When fresh, that natural oil gives mackerel a beautiful flavour, and allows for several different preparations, such as grilling and smoking. Mackerel has another advantage: It is generally very well priced, mostly due to its unpopularity, especially in North America.

Cleaning mackerel is a breeze, as it has a firm, consistent shape, is relatively boneless, and has no scales. You might see Spanish mackerel advertised in addition to Atlantic mackerel. No problem — they are interchangeable, though the Spanish variety tends to be a bit larger. Be aware that "Spanish" just refers to the type of fish and not its origin. It can be from North America, as well. "Horse mackerel," on the other hand, is a completely different fish — also pretty tasty, but more closely related to the "jack" family of fish.

SMOKED MACKEREL DIP

I enjoy the American South. In Florida and Alabama, there is a classic dish: smoked mullet dip. Mullet is another great underused fish (sometimes referred to as "bait fish," like mackerel), but not as commonly seen in fish markets. This is my version of smoked mullet dip, using mackerel.

1 cup (250 mL) salt

2 L (8 cups) cold water

6 to 8 mackerel fillets

250 g (8 oz) cream cheese

Zest of 1 lemon

30 mL (2 tbsp) fresh lemon juice

30 mL (2 tbsp) mayonnaise

30 to 60 mL (2 to 4 tbsp) hot sauce, or to taste

2 shallots, finely minced

60 mL (¼ cup) chives, minced

Salt to taste (optional)

Make a simple brine for the mackerel: Combine salt and cold water in an airtight container large enough to comfortably fit both the fillets and brine (make sure the salt is fully incorporated before adding the fish). Immerse mackerel in brine and refrigerate for about 1.5 hours.

Meanwhile, get your smoker set up, either using a dedicated smoker or a charcoal barbecue, with a small amount of coals off to one side. Mix some chunks of "lighter" wood, such as apple or maple, into the coals. The ideal smoking temperature is about 60°C (140°F).

Remove fish from brine and rinse thoroughly under cold running water. Pat dry with paper towel. (Ideally, the fillets can be further dried in the fridge, on a sheet pan, for another hour or so, until they get a bit sticky, but this is not mandatory.)

Smoke fillets for about 90 minutes. Remove from smoker and let cool.

In a food processor, combine cheese, lemon zest and juice, mayonnaise, hot sauce, and shallots. Pulse for a minute or so, until ingredients start to blend. Pull skin from cooled smoked mackerel, and break fish into the cheese mixture. Pulse for another 2 to 3 minutes, stopping occasionally to scrape down the sides of the food processor (the mixture should be slightly chunky).

Transfer the mixture to a bowl, and stir in chives. The smoked fish will be somewhat salty already, so you may not need any additional salt, but feel free to add salt, if you like. Serve with your favourite crisps/chips.

Makes 450 to 500 g (15 oz to 1 lb) of dip, enough for a nice party of 8 to 10 people

—MENHADEN—

ORIGIN: *East Coast of the United States*
AVAILABILITY: *Year-round*
COMMON FORMS: *Not sold retail or for foodservice*
STOCK STATUS: *Good; management system recently introduced*
SOURCE: *All catch is wild*
ALTERNATIVES: *herring*

POLLOCK IS THE largest fishery in North America by volume, and most people would at least have heard of it. The second largest fishery, though, involves a fish that is almost invisible to consumers: menhaden. Between 600 and 900 million pounds are harvested annually on the East Coast, and have been since the 1970s. Yet you've never been served menhaden at a restaurant, and you've never purchased it or even laid eyes on it at your local fish shop. So, who eats all the menhaden? Where does it go?

Livestock feed, pet food, and fish food, mostly. In fact, we have made use of these docile fish for centuries, even in the crudest of ways, to help us advance. Legend has it that back in the 1600s, early settlers were instructed by Indigenous peoples to plant menhaden alongside their crops as a fertilizer. And while whale oil is thought of as an important product in early North America, menhaden oil production always outstripped that of whale oil. Now, of course, we have refined our practices in terms of extracting value from these fish. Menhaden yields meal and "solubles," for use in animal feeds; and oil, for use in vitamin supplements.

And it's not just us: The ocean is also dependent on menhaden. Like herring, they are one of the biggest converters of plankton into energy, helping to filter wide swaths of the sea. As a forage fish, they in turn are consumed by the piscivorous creatures that surround them: striped bass, bluefin tuna, red snapper, and others.

Happily, so far we seem to have been able to manage the menhaden population pretty well. Purse seining is the most common method of capture, and it results in very low bycatch (one tenth of 1 percent).

PERCH

ORIGIN: *North America, freshwater*
AVAILABILITY: *September to June*
COMMON FORMS: *Fillets, fresh*
STOCK STATUS: *Good, little concern*
SOURCE: *All catch is wild*
ALTERNATIVES: *freshwater bass, red mullet*

YELLOW PERCH IS what we see in North American stores, and the vast majority of it comes from Lake Erie (particularly the western end) and is caught by gillnet or pound (trap) net. The fishery is carefully managed and stable. Usually sold in stores as fillets, perch meat is very delicate, and is a classic Midwest or Great Lakes "fish fry" fish. Some efforts toward cultivation have been undertaken, but the perch farming industry is very small.

LIGHTLY BREADED AND FRIED PERCH

The simplest way to highlight perch is with a light breading and some hot oil. I use chickpea flour with a bit of salt mixed in for my breading. Just fill a pot with 5 to 6 cm (2 to 2½ inches) of oil and heat to about 180°C (350°F). Then drag the fillets through the seasoned flour and carefully immerse them in the hot oil. Fry for 4 to 5 minutes, until golden. Drain on paper towel. Serve with some mayo and lemon. Classic.

━ Hot Perch Sandwich ━

This is my take on the classic hot turkey sandwich. I've always found the bread becomes gloopy and inedible once the gravy is added, so I'm swapping it out for latkes (potato pancakes).

For the potato pancakes:

3 medium potatoes, peeled and grated (use drier baking potatoes or Yukon golds)

30 mL (2 tbsp) all-purpose flour

2 large eggs, whisked

3 to 4 green onions, minced (white and green parts)

Salt and pepper

Vegetable oil, for frying

For the gravy:

125 mL (½ cup) unsalted butter

125 mL (½ cup) all-purpose flour

2 cups (500 mL) milk (2% or whole)

Salt and pepper, to taste

For the peas and fish:

200 mL (¾ cup + 5 tsp) green peas (fresh or frozen)

4 boneless perch fillets (50 to 70 g/1.8 to 2.5 oz per fillet)

Salt, to taste

Avocado or other high-heat oil, for frying

To make the potato pancakes: The grated potatoes will be a little wet. Press them into some cheesecloth to extract the excess moisture or, at the very least, use the back of a wooden spoon to press the potatoes against the bowl, draining as much liquid as you can.

In a bowl, combine grated potatoes and flour. Add whisked eggs and mix well. Stir in the onions, and add salt and pepper.

Preheat oven to 90°C (190°F). Cover a baking sheet in paper towel and place in the preheated oven.

Using a medium sauté pan, over medium heat, heat 1 tsp of oil. After a minute or so, spoon a small amount of the pancake mixture into the pan in the shape of a disk, pushing it together if necessary. Cook for about 4 minutes, then flip and cook the other side for 3 minutes. Remove from heat, test pancake for seasoning, and adjust batter if necessary. Finish frying the remaining batter, making 4- to 6-cm (1½- to 2½-inch) pancakes, about 1 cm (½ inch) thick. You should end up with 4 to 6 pancakes. Place pancakes on baking sheet and return to oven to keep warm.

To make the gravy: In a small saucepan over medium-low heat, melt butter. Whisk in four and cook, whisking constantly, until it turns light brown. Add about half of the milk, and keep whisking. Once milk is fully incorporated, gradually whisk in the remaining milk. Remove from heat, and add salt and pepper, to your taste. The gravy should be fairly peppery. Keep warm on very low heat.

To cook the peas and fish: Put a small pot of salted water on to boil. Once water is boiling, add peas and cook just until they turn bright green, about 3 minutes. Remove from heat and drain peas. Set aside.

Meanwhile, in a medium sauté pan over medium-high heat, add 30 to 45 mL (2 to 3 tbsp) oil. When the oil starts to shimmer, salt the fillets and lay them in the pan. Cook for 3 minutes or so, then turn over and cook the other side for about 2 minutes. The skin of this very delicate fish will turn crispy, with the edges taking on a bit of dark char. The clear white flesh will quickly turn opaque. Stir some of the pan juices into the peas.

Divide the pancakes between two serving plates, keeping the pancakes tight together. Lay the fish on top, and then pour a nice amount of gravy over the fish. Finally, top with the peas.

Serves 2

The skin of this very delicate fish will turn crispy, with the edges taking on a bit of dark char. The clear white flesh will quickly turn opaque.

‑Red Mullet‑

ORIGIN: *Northeast Atlantic, Mediterranean Sea*
AVAILABILITY: *Mostly year-round, lower from April to August*
COMMON FORMS: *Whole*
STOCK STATUS: *Good, little concern*
SOURCE: *All catch is wild*
ALTERNATIVES: *perch, whiting*

NOT TO BE confused with the grey mullet of the Southeastern United States, this small, slim fish with a beautiful reddish-pink skin is found throughout Europe, primarily along the Atlantic coast of the United Kingdom and France, as well as in the Mediterranean Sea, especially the Turkish and Tunisian regions. Also known as rouget, red mullet has a long history as a pet in Europe: Apparently, these fish can be trained (slowly) to come at the sound of a bell. In Roman times, during the reign of Tiberius, they would be sold at auction individually. According to the Roman gourmet and writer Apicius, each fish could fetch more than the equivalent of $1,000 in today's currency.

Similar in size to sardines or perch, they can be filleted or poached, as in the classic bouillabaisse, but are perfect for frying or grilling whole. Scale the fish, but take care to keep the skin intact, as it will crisp up beautifully, and is truly fatty and delicious. The flesh is fairly firm, with a very sweet, almost "shellfish" flavour.

When cleaning the fish, hang on to the liver, if possible, as it can be put back into the body while grilling. Or for a beautiful spread, quickly sauté it and then purée with some olives, garlic, and herbs.

ALPHABET SOUP: WHAT DO ALL OF THE CERTIFICATIONS MEAN AND WHO ARE THESE PEOPLE, ANYWAY?

You've undoubtedly seen the signs and logos on menus and in stores: Ocean Wise, Seafood Watch, MSC. These are just a few of the seafood-certifying bodies that have sprung up over the past 20 years. This is not a complete list, but it demonstrates a couple of things: first, that ocean health and fish population stability is being taken more seriously than ever; and second, that because there are so many of these groups, they might not all see eye to eye. Ironically, this often makes determining the best fish to buy more difficult for the average person.

Even though many of these organizations have given themselves a quasi-governmental air, it's important to remember that most of them are private organizations that depend on donations from individuals, foundations, and even from the fishing industry. This can obviously lead to conflicting, inaccurate, or confusing information. Governments play a role in studying ocean health, but as consumers, you are far more likely to encounter these private certifications.

The three groups I mention above are the most quoted organizations in North America regarding the status of a particular fish stock. Ocean Wise and Seafood Watch are products of aquariums on the West Coast, and are privately funded. They tend to assess fisheries on a regular basis, or if someone brings a concern to their attention. They're reasonably thorough, and they agree on a lot of things. If their stamp is on a particular fish, it's probably A-okay, but absence of their approval doesn't necessarily mean that you shouldn't buy it. MSC tends to be a little more industry-driven, with individual fisheries, or co-operatives, applying to be assessed and typically paying a fee to cover at least part of the process. Once a fishery is MSC-certified, it is likely to be a well-managed fishery, but the certification process takes time, and sometimes a fish that might be perfectly okay gets stuck in the assessment pipeline.

So how do you make sense of all of this? Certainly if there is some sort of approval listed from one of these groups, you can buy with confidence. If you don't necessarily see those labels, but the person behind the counter, or the server at the table, can give you some detailed information about the fish, you can likely trust them. But that's what it all boils down to: trust. Any piece of fish can be placed on ice and called anything the vendor wants. It's definitely harder to pass off a piece of sole as snapper, but there are a lot of easy substitutions out there. The butcher case is no different. How do you really know that a piece of beef came from that particular farm? You just have to trust.

The fact that there are so many high-profile organizations making an impact is a positive sign. But if our goal is to maintain a diverse food supply for generations to come, we need to continue to support the efforts of all these entities.

Better food tends to cost more. This isn't an absolute, of course — you can still fall victim to the law of diminishing returns with products like Wagyu beef, for example — but real change, in terms of what distributors will import, only happens when retailers and restaurants ask for better product. If consumers request better fish (that is, certified fish) and accept that it will be a bit pricier, the requests to the distributors will reflect that, and eventually the mix of seafood will shift toward a better supply. It won't happen overnight, but it has already begun.

Ask for certified fish whenever possible, or develop a strong relationship with your local fish shop so you can feel comfortable that they are giving you solid information and are themselves being careful about what they buy.

SARDINE

ORIGIN: *Worldwide*

AVAILABILITY: *Year-round*

COMMON FORMS: *Whole, frozen; canned*

STOCK STATUS: *Good, some concerns, especially in Eastern Pacific (British Columbia and Northwestern United States)*

SOURCE: *All catch is wild*

ALTERNATIVES: *herring, whiting*

IF SOMEONE ASKED if you'd ever eaten a pilchard, you'd probably say "no." Most people have never even heard of a pilchard. But "sardine" is just another name for a juvenile pilchard or herring. Usually smaller than 10 to 12.5 cm (4 to 5 inches) long, sardines are often referred to as a "forage fish," which means that they feed all kinds of other animals, as well as us. Happily, many of the sardine fisheries are relatively healthy, with the recent exception of the Pacific North American fishery, which closed a few years ago due to stock collapse. Both environmental issues (insufficient plankton) and overfishing are being blamed for this, and it has been a massive blow to the fisheries in California and British Columbia. Some estimate it could be another decade before stocks recover.

Sardines are relatively bony, though the bones are fine and the flesh lifts away easily when cooked. They are also high in oils, which gives them a rich, deep flavour (fun fact: sardine oil used to be extracted to lubricate machinery). Most frequently purchased canned or frozen, they are very perishable when fresh.

—SMELTS—

ORIGIN: *Canada, United States, Chile*
AVAILABILITY: *Year-round, though typically October to March in North America*
COMMON FORMS: *Whole, head removed, gutted*
STOCK STATUS: *Good, no major concerns*
SOURCE: *All catch is wild*
ALTERNATIVES: *herring*

SMELT SHACKS ARE a common sight on the frozen waters around New Brunswick in the colder months. It's like a trailer park for winter-loving fishers. Although freshwater lake smelts are available, the main commercial fishery is salt water. Fresh smelt availability starts in October, but prime time is from January until May.

Usually sold as whole fish, though cleaned and headed, they have a mild, almost cucumber smell when fresh. The classic preparation is to simply roll them in flour and fry in oil, then serve with a side of tartar sauce. The bones and spine are tender enough to eat, so no special cleaning is needed other than a quick rinse under cold running water.

— PICKLED SMELTS —

My background is Polish, so pickled herring is a steady presence in my mom's fridge.
I find it harder to get good herring than smelts, so I've developed this method for
pickling smelts instead. The smelts turn out beautifully firm and white.

60 mL (¼ cup) coarse or pickling salt

1.25 L (5 cups) water, divided

450 g (1 lb) whole smelts, headed
and gutted

500 mL (2 cups) apple cider vinegar

60 mL (¼ cup) granulated sugar

3 shallots, sliced

30 mL (2 tbsp) fresh lemon juice

2 bay leaves

10 whole black peppercorns

In a large bowl, combine salt and 1 L (4 cups) of the water; stir until the salt is fully dissolved. Cut smelts into 2-cm (¾-inch) chunks and immerse in brine. Refrigerate overnight, but no more than 24 hours.

Meanwhile, make the pickling juice: In a saucepan, combine cider vinegar and remaining 250 mL (1 cup) water and bring to a boil. Add sugar and stir until completely dissolved. Remove from heat and let cool to room temperature. Add shallots, lemon juice, bay leaves, and pepper. Set aside.

Transfer smelts from original brine to one large (2 L/8 cups) glass container, or divide evenly between a few smaller jars; discard salt brine. Pour prepared pickling juice overtop, until fish are covered. If you don't have enough pickling juice, just make a little more liquid, using the ratio of two parts vinegar to one part water, with a little sugar. Cover and refrigerate. It'll keep for 3 to 4 weeks.

Serves 4 to 6 as a snack with some toasts

WHITING

ORIGIN: *Both Eastern and Western Atlantic,
Mediterranean Sea*

AVAILABILITY: *Year-round*

COMMON FORMS: *Whole*

STOCK STATUS: *Very good overall, especially in North America,
where quotas are rarely reached due to low demand; strong European
management has led to stable stocks, though low*

SOURCE: *All catch is wild*

ALTERNATIVES: *perch, haddock, branzino*

THESE LONG, SLENDER fish are also known as silver hake, a member of the cod and haddock family. Fished on both the East and West coasts of North America, the fish biomass is pretty healthy; it's the fishery that is not so well supported, especially on the East Coast. Fishers can get as little as 5 cents a pound for their catch — hardly enough to cover their fuel costs for running the boat. It's a shame, because whiting is very tasty, and not that different from cod. Due to their shape, taking fillets from the fish gives you a smaller yield, but they are terrific grilled whole, and very inexpensive. Due to the delicacy of their flesh, whiting are perfect for applications like fish cakes, pâté, or brandade. They're also a nice, inexpensive option for making fish stock, as they are a lower-oil whitefish. They really are a great example of an underappreciated fish.

ROE

ORIGIN: *Worldwide*

AVAILABILITY: *Year-round*

COMMON FORMS: *Cured, ready to eat, canned and bottled*

STOCK STATUS: *Very dependent on species used; avoid wild ossetra, sevruga, beluga; also tobiko (flying fish), due to its typically unclear country of origin*

SOURCE: *Almost all sturgeon eggs are farmed; most other roe is wild*

ALTERNATIVES: *Feel free to substitute eggs: paddlefish and whitefish eggs are smaller; trout eggs are larger*

SO MANY PEOPLE overlook fish eggs (roe). It doesn't always have to be the outlandishly priced ossetra or beluga sturgeon eggs. In fact, it's probably better to avoid these two altogether, as the pressure on those particular fish stocks has nearly wiped out the fish. There are so many other great fish egg options: whitefish, salmon, trout, mullet, paddlefish, to name a few. There are even cultivated sturgeon eggs from British Columbia and New Brunswick that, to me, are every bit as good as the "real" stuff.

Another great thing about fish eggs is that they freeze pretty well, so buying a jar of frozen whitefish or trout caviar is still going to give you a very satisfying result, with firm eggs and a clean flavour. Some countries include additives (related to Borax), known as E284 and E285, in their caviar. Check the label closely, and avoid caviar with these preservatives. They will certainly extend shelf life, but at the expense of texture, flavour, and potentially your health.

Bottarga is another way to use fish eggs. It's simply a skein (egg sac) that has been kept intact and cured more intensively than caviar, until it becomes quite solid. The bottarga can then be shaved or thinly sliced and used to add depth of flavour to a dish.

MAKING CAVIAR AT HOME

Caviar is roe that has been salted or "cured." The lack of processing is beautiful, and the technique is so simple: In a bowl, combine 3 L (12 cups) of room-temperature water with about 250 mL (1 cup) of non-iodized salt. Place the whole skein (the entire sac of eggs, including the thin membrane that surrounds them) into the brine and let sit for about 30 minutes. Remove skein (reserve brine), and make an incision in it. Push the eggs into a fine-mesh sieve, removing as much of the membrane from the eggs as possible. Rinse the eggs well under cold running water. Place the eggs back into the reserved brine and let soak for 3 to 5 minutes, until they've reached the desired saltiness. And that's it. Spoon the eggs into a glass jar and refrigerate for up to 10 days.

— BUCKWHEAT BLINI —

Personally, I feel that the simpler your caviar "set up" is the better. Spooning it directly onto the back of your hand, and following it with a shot of wine or well-chilled vodka is perfectly acceptable. I understand, however, that you won't always be in a situation where your guests will feel comfortable just using their hands. A couple of things on the side couldn't hurt. Buckwheat blini make a great alternate medium to your hands.

325 mL (1⅓ cups) bread flour or
　　all-purpose flour

150 mL (⅔ cup) buckwheat flour

5 mL (1 tsp) baking powder

5 mL (1 tsp) fine salt

200 mL (¾ cup + 5 tsp) whole milk, at
　　room temperature

30 mL (2 tbsp) melted butter

1 large egg, at room temperature

Additional butter, for melting in the pan

In a medium bowl, whisk together flours, baking powder, and salt, ensuring everything is combined evenly.

In a separate bowl, whisk together milk, butter, and egg. Gradually stir into flour mixture, trying to eliminate lumps. The batter should be a pouring consistency, but not runny. If it seems a little thick, don't worry about it just yet. Let it sit, covered, for about 30 minutes to let the flour absorb the liquid completely. If after that it still seems a little thick, add a splash of milk and stir until you reach the desired consistency.

Place a plate in the oven, and preheat oven to about 80°C (170°F).

In a medium sauté pan, over medium-low heat, add about a teaspoon of butter. When it starts to bubble, swirl it around so butter covers the bottom of the pan. Then, using a small ladle, drop some batter in the pan. Each blini should be about 3 cm (1¼ inches) in diameter, so fit as many into the pan as is comfortable, likely 3 to 4. Cook for about 2 minutes, then turn over and cook the other side for a minute or so, until blini is cooked through. Transfer cooked blini to the plate in the oven to keep warm. Repeat until all batter is used. I find it's best to wipe the pan clean with a dry paper towel between batches.

Makes 12 to 15 blini

OTHER THINGS THAT CAN BE SERVED ALONGSIDE YOUR CAVIAR:

- *Crème fraîche or sour cream — Please ensure that you are getting high-quality stuff. Many sour creams have a lot of needless additives. True sour cream needs only milk, bacterial culture, and microbial enzymes.*
- *Minced chives, not green onions*
- *Boiled, peeled, and halved new potatoes*
- *Minced red onions tossed in cider vinegar*

MEDIUM FISH

This section covers the bulk of the fish you are likely to find at a fish shop or on a menu. Medium-size fish tend to be the most common commercial species, both wild and farmed. Because it's such a large category, pricing, fish stock health, and availability are all over the map. Some historic favourites (for example, cod and haddock) have given way to new equivalents (basa, tilapia, and rockfish), which are not always great choices. Through careful stock management and progress in farming techniques, the alternatives are getting better and some classics are slowly returning. These fish, even though many of them are considered workhorses, require us to be even more diligent if we are to enjoy them for years to come.

I recommend buying whole fish whenever possible, though I understand it can be a bit of a hassle. I love the crackle of the skin, the juice just beneath that skin, and the unique experience of whole-fish dining. Food memories are important, and a fillet can't hold a candle to the whole fish in the "memorable" department. Of course, I won't tell you how to dine. I just can't help letting my prejudices creep through sometimes.

Don't sleep on lake fish. They are some of the best value, truly local, and historically important fish available, especially in the middle of the continent. They're also delicious. We invariably sell more ocean than lake fish, even in Toronto, and while I expect that to continue, it would be great to see a stronger showing from the freshwater species going forward.

For advice on handling and storage, see page 277.

―Albacore Tuna―

ORIGIN: *Worldwide*

AVAILABILITY: *Year-round*

COMMON FORMS: *Fillets, fresh and frozen*

STOCK STATUS: *Some concern; best to focus on North American Pacific, as it is well managed*

SOURCE: *All catch is wild*

ALTERNATIVES: *yellowfin tuna, kingfish, mackerel*

IF TUNA IS your goal, albacore should be your aim. The Pacific albacore fishery is the best managed of all the various tuna fisheries. Much of what is available is in a frozen "loin" format, which is a low-waste and easy-to-handle piece of fish. Since it is frozen quickly and well, it is perfect for sushi/sashimi/tartare. Of course, it can also be seared or smoked, among many other choices, but certainly the less you mess with it, the more you will let the sweet, subtle flavour shine through.

── ALBACORE TARTARE ──

Tartare is a very simple way to prepare raw fish. Now widely used in restaurants, albacore tuna has replaced the less readily available and more expensive bluefin tuna, so it's pretty easy to find. Ginger and lime provide a lovely fresh flavour, making this the ideal starter for a summer dinner.

60 mL (¼ cup) crystallized
   turbinado sugar

45 mL (3 tbsp) fish sauce

Juice from 2 limes

Juice from 1 small chunk of
   peeled ginger

1 cayenne pepper, seeded and diced

1 small bunch of fresh coriander,
   leaves, stems, and roots finely
   chopped

1 clove garlic, crushed and minced

Salt, to taste

300 to 400 g (10.5 to 14 oz) albacore
   tuna loin, cut into ½-cm (¼-inch)
   cubes

In a bowl, combine sugar, fish sauce, lime juice, ginger juice, diced cayenne pepper, chopped coriander, and minced garlic. Mix together using a metal spoon, occasionally crushing mixture against the side of the bowl to release more flavour. Taste and add salt, if needed. Add cubed tuna and stir gently. Taste. If acidity is low, squeeze a bit more lime juice into the mixture. Serve with small toasts.

Serves 4 to 6 as an appetizer

ALFONSINO

ORIGIN: *New Zealand*
AVAILABILITY: *Year-round*
COMMON FORMS: *Whole*
STOCK STATUS: *Good, little concern*
SOURCE: *All catch is wild*
ALTERNATIVES: *snapper, bream*

LARGELY FISHED OFF the coast of New Zealand, this red snapper lookalike can also be found in Southern Atlantic waters, though it is rarely targeted. Due to the general lack of demand, alfonsino hasn't been closely studied. The International Union for Conservation of Nature (IUCN) lists it as a species of "least concern." SeaChoice and Ocean Wise are okay with certain fish from managed areas using the midwater trawl and longline methods. MSC hasn't assessed the stocks at all. The alfonsino is a poster child for the limitations of our current advisory systems, as we are given highly conflicting advice about whether we should be eating this delicious fish.

I lean toward promoting regulated consumption of alfonsino. Certainly, methods such as bottom trawling are not at all recommended, but outside of that, and in waters that are being overseen by the New Zealand and Australian governments — where the majority of alfonsino is currently sourced — I think it's safe to eat a certain amount.

The fish itself is beautiful, with shiny orange-red skin and big deep eyes. Its fairly delicate flesh does well in more gentle preparations, and is tremendous to eat raw or in a ceviche. Some processors (Lee Fish, NZ, for example) offer fish that have been killed using the *ike jime* method, which involves pulling the fish, still living, from the longline, and inserting a needle directly into the back of its head, killing it instantly and as gently as possible. The alfonsino is then bled immediately. This method is said to produce the highest-quality flesh, especially for use at the raw bar.

Alfonsino has some small scales, which should be removed, especially if you plan to eat the skin, which is delicious. If you are not confident with filleting such a delicate fish, roast it whole. If you are able to generate fillets, sear it until the skin is crisp, and then let the residual heat finish off the skinless side. So simple and so tasty.

AMBERJACK

ORIGIN: *Japan, Gulf of Mexico, New Zealand*

AVAILABILITY: *Year-round*

COMMON FORMS: *Fillets, fresh and frozen*

STOCK STATUS: *Serious problems with Japanese-sourced fish;
ensure this fish is sourced from either the United States or New Zealand;
look for other fish in the "jack" family as well*

SOURCE: *Most catch is wild; some farmed fish is available but not recommended*

ALTERNATIVES: *Any "jack" family member, New Zealand yellowtail, kingfish*

MOST COMMONLY SEEN in sushi restaurants, amberjack (yellowtail or hamachi) is often thought of as a tuna, but it is actually unrelated. Almost all of the amberjack that we see is imported from Japan, and it's a problematic fishery in that country. The vast majority of Japanese amberjack comes from ranching operations, which source their fry or juvenile fish from the wild. They are then grown to maturity in net pens. Unfortunately, because these producers rely on an already taxed wild stock for their juvenile fish, they are not really helping fish stocks, as is the intention of aquaculture.

If you can find U.S.-sourced amberjack — or other fish from the "jack" family, such as trevally — then by all means avail yourself of this beautiful fish. Another good option comes from New Zealand, where yellowtail is also referred to as "kingfish."

Handle amberjack as you would other rich fish — simply grilled or served raw — so as not to allow the natural fattiness to go to waste.

Arctic Char

ORIGIN: *Arctic, North Atlantic*

AVAILABILITY: *Year-round*

COMMON FORMS: *Whole; fillets*

STOCK STATUS: *Small amount of wild harvest is well managed; most catch is farmed*

SOURCE: *Most char is farmed; a small amount of wild catch is available in the far northern regions of Canada, mostly in the spring*

ALTERNATIVES: *trout, salmon*

HISTORICALLY A VERY important species for northern Indigenous peoples, wild char is rarely seen in fish shops or restaurants any more. A few fisheries have been certified, such as Cambridge Bay in Nunavut, but the vast majority of char available today is farmed. Landing somewhere between salmon and trout in terms of flesh and taste, char has a gorgeous fattiness and a fine-grained meat. It's no wonder that it is still highly prized even when farmed.

In the Aroostook Valley in northern Maine, a few small populations of char are still around, a legacy of glacial retreat. It's rare to see them so far south, and these populations are highly controlled.

Recreational fishing is the only way to procure these, usually in late June or October. If you're craving a great fishing experience and a fantastic fish, this might be something to put on your bucket list.

Char tends to be fairly slimy, and must be rinsed off before cooking. This coating is somewhat stubborn, so it might need a bit of a wipe in addition to the water. You are most likely to find fillets at your local shop, so roasting whole char is probably not an option. The fact that it is shipped filleted reduces its shelf life somewhat, so look for fillets that aren't gaping, and ensure that the slime on the fish looks and smells fresh, not dried or funky.

Arctic Char with Savoury Clam Sauce

I love the combination of this somewhat fatty fish and the brininess of these little clams. The juices come together in the pan to produce something much greater than the sum of its parts. I like to add something green to the mix as well. If you're preparing this dish in late spring or early summer, fresh peas are perfect. In other times of the year, try asparagus, Brussels sprouts, or rapini.

4 skin-on char fillets (about 175 g/6 oz each)

Salt and pepper, to taste

45 mL (3 tbsp) unsalted butter

1 shallot, minced

300 g (10 oz) shiitake mushrooms, torn into strips

30 mL (2 tbsp) grapeseed oil

200 mL (¾ cup + 5 tsp) dry white wine

2 sprigs fresh thyme, picked

400 to 500 g (14 to 16 oz) B.C. savoury clams (see Tip)

250 mL (1 cup) fresh peas

Sprinkle a generous amount of salt and pepper on both sides of char fillets, and place them, skin-side up, on a plate to let the skin dry out just a little.

Preheat oven to 160°C (325°F).

In a medium saucepan with a lid, over low heat, melt butter. Add minced shallot and cook, stirring occasionally, for about 5 minutes, until softened. Toss in the mushrooms and stir to coat in the melted butter. Cover the pot, and simmer for 5 to 8 minutes.

Meanwhile, in a skillet, over medium-high heat, heat oil until it shimmers. Place prepared fish in the pan, skin-side down, and let cook, undisturbed, for about 4 minutes, until the skin is slightly brown around the edges and crisp looking. Place fish, skin-side up, on a baking sheet. Bake in preheated oven for about 5 minutes (the flesh of the fish will have turned a much lighter pink, but it's fine to leave it a bit bright in the centre).

Add white wine to the mushroom/shallot mixture, along with the thyme. Increase heat to high. When wine is bubbling, add clams to pot and cover. Cook for 3 minutes, and then add peas. Cover and remove pot from heat.

Remove fish from oven and divide evenly among 4 serving plates. Add an even number of clams to each plate, discarding any that haven't opened. Spoon the mushrooms, peas, and resulting sauce overtop of the fish and clams. Add salt and pepper, to your taste.

Serves 4 as a main course

TIP
If you can't find B.C. savoury clams, you can substitute Manila clams or small littleneck clams.

—BARRAMUNDI—

ORIGIN: *Australia, United States, Vietnam/Southeast Asia*
AVAILABILITY: *Year-round*
COMMON FORMS: *Whole; fillets*
STOCK STATUS: *Good, little concern, though best to look for U.S.-farmed barramundi*
SOURCE: *Most is now farmed; about 25 percent is of wild origin*
ALTERNATIVES: *striped bass, branzino*

MOST FAMOUSLY AN Australian fish, barramundi (or Asian seabass) is now available in North America via a couple of aquaculture operations in the eastern United States. The U.S. fish are of very high quality, and as they are related to other seabass, they lend themselves to many preparations. In the wild, barramundi can grow to more than 45 kg (100 lb), but cultivated versions rarely exceed 3 kg (7 lb) or so.

Although the fish is practically iconic in Australia, the truth is that the wild fishery produces only about 20 percent of that country's demand for barramundi. Another 25 to 30 percent is generated by Australian aquaculture, with the rest coming from countries such as Vietnam, Malaysia, India, and Indonesia. This has created friction among Australian producers, who feel that consumers are being misled and are paying for substandard fish. A similar uproar is taking place in the United States among domestic catfish producers, who are worried about less expensive Asian imports squeezing out domestic supply.

Wild vs. Farmed Fish

Having worked with fish for so long, I've overheard a lot of questionable declarations over the years:

"I only eat wild fish."

"Farmed fish contains too many chemicals, and I'm allergic."

"I want sustainable fish, but it has to be wild."

The irony, of course, is that every other protein we eat is farmed, and has been for a long time. Sure, you might eat the occasional deer or moose that you shot yourself, but it's a tiny portion of the meat you consume. There are no wild alternatives to beef, chicken, or pork, and most of us are completely okay with that. So why is there such a pushback against farmed fish? The most obvious answer is that we can still access wild fish and that it just feels better, psychologically, to insist on something we perceive to be more "natural."

The truth is we still have access to wild fish only because we weren't able to catch them all before we wised up. Over the last few thousand years, it was a lot easier to conquer the land than the ocean. It's still true, though we are trying our best, even now, to extract everything we can from the ocean. It's only been in the last 30 to 40 years that we have really gotten serious about any sort of conservation in the various fisheries. Canada, for instance, recently celebrated a big anniversary: 25 years ago, in July 1992, John Crosbie, Federal Minister of Fisheries, declared a moratorium on the fishing of northern cod. And only recently have the cod stocks shown any sign of a significant rebound.

There are no wild alternatives to beef, chicken, or pork, and most of us are completely okay with that. So why is there such a pushback against farmed fish?

Happily, fish farming has a tremendous presence in the marketplace. In fact, farmed fish now represent over 50 percent of all seafood harvested and consumed. This takes pressure off the remaining wild stocks and ensures that we will have fish in the long term. We now have organizations such as the Marine Stewardship Council (MSC), Ocean Wise, and the Monterey Bay Aquarium, to name a few, that are trying to monitor and assess wild stocks. They apply labels to various fisheries — "least concern," "threatened," "avoid," etc. — in an attempt to guide consumers and chefs toward good choices. This is certainly helpful, but it's really just a best guess. It's almost impossible to get a perfect understanding of all the pressures on the various fish stocks. They certainly do their best to stock good choices of wild fish at Honest Weight, and I have a deep appreciation for wild fish. But if we are truly talking about a sustainable future for fish and seafood, then farming has to be a major part of that conversation.

For many years (until quite recently, really), we weren't overly concerned with how our chickens or pigs or cows were treated before they got to the butcher shop or grocery store. Price was (and, let's be honest, still is) the primary criterion when making the decision to purchase. Today, we are seeing the rise of more thoughtful farming practices — cage-free, raised without hormones — and it's a great trend. But just as we are now able to differentiate between good and bad farming practices on the land, we need to start making the same distinctions for aquaculture.

Aquaculture has had both the misfortune and opportunity to develop in a more environmentally conscious era, one in which the media has focused on food production

BONITO

ORIGIN: *Western and Eastern Atlantic, Eastern Pacific*
AVAILABILITY: *Year-round*
COMMON FORMS: *Fillets*
STOCK STATUS: *Good, little concern*
SOURCE: *All catch is wild*
ALTERNATIVES: *mackerel, Spanish mackerel, kingfish*

BONITO IS A beautiful fish, both aesthetically and from a flavour standpoint. It comes from the mackerel family, but it's the size of a small tuna, and often gets substituted for skipjack or albacore tuna. The flesh is a deep ruby colour, firm, and with a rich flavour that lends itself to more aggressive preparations, such as grilling or smoking. The fish reproduce at a younger age than tuna, and the fishery is well managed, so it's a good choice, no matter what you decide to do with it.

KATSUOBUSHI

Though you won't often see bonito in fish shops, you have almost certainly eaten it. Dried, smoked, and fermented bonito, known as "katsuobushi," is one of the building blocks of Japanese cooking. It is a key — and sometimes only — ingredient in dashi (see recipe page 91), the broth that gives so many dishes their depth of flavour (umami). Unlike beef or chicken stock, making dashi is a quick and easy process. This is because katsuobushi, the main ingredient, has already been laboured over for many months. The bonito is filleted, boiled, deboned, and then put into a smoker on and off for about a month. At this point, the dried fish is referred to as "arabushi," and usually comes shaved, bagged, and sold as a garnish or dashi ingredient. If the producer is interested in creating something even more intense and valuable, the fillets will then be inoculated with a mould, similar to the one used in the sake-making process. The fish is then alternately left in the sun and kept indoors for up to 6 months, sometimes more. It then earns the grades of "karebushi" or "honkarebushi," and is typically sold whole. The fillets, at this point, have lost over 80 percent of their original water and weight, and resemble wood. They are shaved using a special planer that very closely resembles a carpenter's plane.

BREAM

ORIGIN: *Northeast Atlantic, Mediterranean, Black Sea, as bream; Northwest Atlantic, as porgy*
AVAILABILITY: *Year-round*
COMMON FORMS: *Whole*
STOCK STATUS: *Good, little concern*
SOURCE: *Most catch is farmed; some wild fish available*
ALTERNATIVES: *porgy, ocean perch, snapper*

A COMMONLY SEEN and well-regarded smaller fish, reminiscent of sea bass but more tender, bream is often called daurade royale, dorada, and besugo, as well as gilthead bream in North America. Another North American version of this fish is better known as porgy, scup, or sheepshead. A small amount of wild-fished bream is still available, but most product purchased in North America is cultivated, some from Canada, but mostly from Europe (Cyprus, France, Greece, Iceland, Israel, Italy, and Spain).

Due to its size when aquacultured (generally 400 to 600 g/14 to 21 oz), and relatively tender texture, bream is best cooked whole or presented as ceviche. Fillets taken from the fish are quite small, especially after cooking. As the whole fish tends to be well priced, I recommend serving one fish per person. If you are using it for ceviche, definitely go with 2 to 3, folks.

Overall, bream is not the most exciting fish around, but it is a solid choice. It's not under any threat of overfishing, especially if you're purchasing aquaculture product.

DEEP-FRIED BREAM WITH RICE AND NAM JIM SAUCE

*A 300 to 400 g (10.5 to 14 oz) fish makes a perfect meal for one person, but it is
a bit of a hassle to fillet. When you fry the whole fish, the flesh lifts off the bones easily.
The cooked fish has an addictive quality that quickly overcomes the hassle of eating around the
bones. Be sure to score the fish down to the bone at least a couple of times on each
side to allow the oil to penetrate more thoroughly.*

For the nam jim sauce:

45 mL (3 tbsp) cane sugar

15 mL (1 tbsp) salt + more to finish

Zest and juice of 3 limes

20 mL (4 tsp) fish sauce

1 bunch fresh coriander, stems and
leaves separated

3 green onions, cut into rings
(use all of the white parts and about
half of the green)

2 cayenne chilies, split, seeded, ribbed,
and finely minced

For the bream:

2 L (8 cups) vegetable oil

2 whole bream (300 to 400 g/10.5 to
14 oz each), scaled and cleaned, at
room temperature

250 mL (1 cup) long-grain rice, cooked

To make the nam jim sauce: In a bowl, combine sugar, salt, lime zest and
juice, and fish sauce. Whisk until sugar and salt are dissolved. Using a
sharp knife, finely mince the coriander stems and add to the mixture
along with the green onions and chilies. Set aside.

To fry the fish: In a pot large enough to fit at least one fish, heat oil to
190°C (375°F) — if you have a pot big enough to fit both, even better.
Carefully add the fish (remember to score the sides first) to the hot oil
and fry for about 10 minutes. Flip gently and cook the other side for an
additional 5 minutes. If you can only cook one fish at a time, keep the
first cooked fish warm on a wire rack in a preheated 80°C (170°F) oven
until ready to eat. Cook second fish in same way.

Remove cooked fish from oil, and let drain briefly on paper towel.
Serve with rice and nam jim sauce. Garnish with coriander leaves.

Serves 2

CARP

ORIGIN: *Worldwide*

AVAILABILITY: *Year-round*

COMMON FORMS: *Whole; fillets*

STOCK STATUS: *Good, little concern*

SOURCE: *All catch is wild*

ALTERNATIVES: *grouper, catfish*

CARP IS NOT indigenous to North American waters. It was first introduced by European colonists in the mid-1800s and later by the U.S. government. But since the carp has no native predators, what began as a relatively innocent experiment blossomed into a disaster by 1900, as the common carp overwhelmed many native freshwater game fish and destroyed many aquatic habitats. Large-scale removal and poisoning efforts failed, though recently the population seems to have stabilized, and efforts are underway to encourage carp consumption to further control things.

Knowing what we do about carp's ability and willingness to proliferate, one would think we'd have learned our lesson. Not so. In the mid-1970s, so-called "Asian carp" — actually a variety of carp species, including silver, grass, bighead, and black — were introduced to Arkansas to control algae growth in early aquaculture operations. Disaster struck, flooding occurred, and a few Asian carp found their way into the watershed. Today, they can be found in over 30 states, and there is a massive effort underway to prevent their spread into the Great Lakes, where it is feared that they will decimate the commercial and sport fishing industries, worth almost $1 billion annually. The U.S. Army Corp's of Engineers is even trying underwater electric fencing, with limited success.

So should we develop a taste for carp? It would certainly help the North American aquatic environment. But Honest Weight doesn't carry carp; if it were on the menu, it wouldn't sell. Yet there it is: a fully sustainable, invasive species that is, by many accounts, reasonably tasty. I've even got a pretty delicious recipe for carp (see next page). But I can pretty much guarantee it will never be cooked — and carp will never be popular in North America.

⎯ ALSATIAN-STYLE DOUBLE-FRIED CARP ⎯ WITH STEAMED POTATOES AND WILTED GREENS

Old-world fried carp — plain, simple, and delicious.

For the fried carp:

4 carp fillets (150 to 175 g/5 oz to 6 oz each), skin off

500 mL (2 cups) dry white wine

250 mL (1 cup) finely ground semolina flour

1 L (4 cups) vegetable oil, for frying

Salt and pepper, to taste

For the potatoes and greens:

8 medium potatoes, peeled

125 mL (½ cup) unsalted butter

50 mL (3 tbsp + 1 tsp) white wine vinegar

30 mL (2 tbsp) Dijon mustard

15 mL (1 tbsp) granulated sugar

500 mL (2 cups) Swiss chard, lightly chopped

250 mL (1 cup) baby bok choy, lightly chopped

Salt, to taste

Small handful chopped fresh dill

Lemon wedges

To make the fried carp: Pour white wine into a non-reactive dish or bowl and submerge fish. Cover and refrigerate for 2 to 4 hours. Remove fish from marinade (discard marinade) and pat dry with paper towel. Set aside.

Place flour in a shallow dish. In a pot big enough to accommodate two fillets at a time, heat oil to 160°C (325°F).

Generously season marinated fish with salt and pepper, and dredge both sides in the flour.

Carefully place fillets (two at a time) into the hot oil. Fry for about 3 minutes per side. Transfer cooked fish to a wire rack to drain. Repeat with the remaining fillets. Reserve hot oil.

To make the greens and potatoes: Start steaming the potatoes in a double boiler for about 20 minutes. About halfway through the steaming time, start cooking greens: In a sauté pan over low heat, combine butter, vinegar, mustard, and sugar; cover pan and bring to a boil. Uncover and increase heat to medium-high, then add a splash of water and greens. Cover, and let cook for 4 to 5 minutes, until greens have wilted. Remove from heat. When potatoes are tender, gently crush them with a fork and stir them into the cooked greens. Add salt, to your taste.

Heat reserved oil to 190°C (375°F). Re-fry fish for 2 minutes per side. Quickly drain fish on a paper towel. Plate double-fried fish with a side of the greens and potatoes. Garnish with fresh dill and lemon.

Serves 4 as a main course

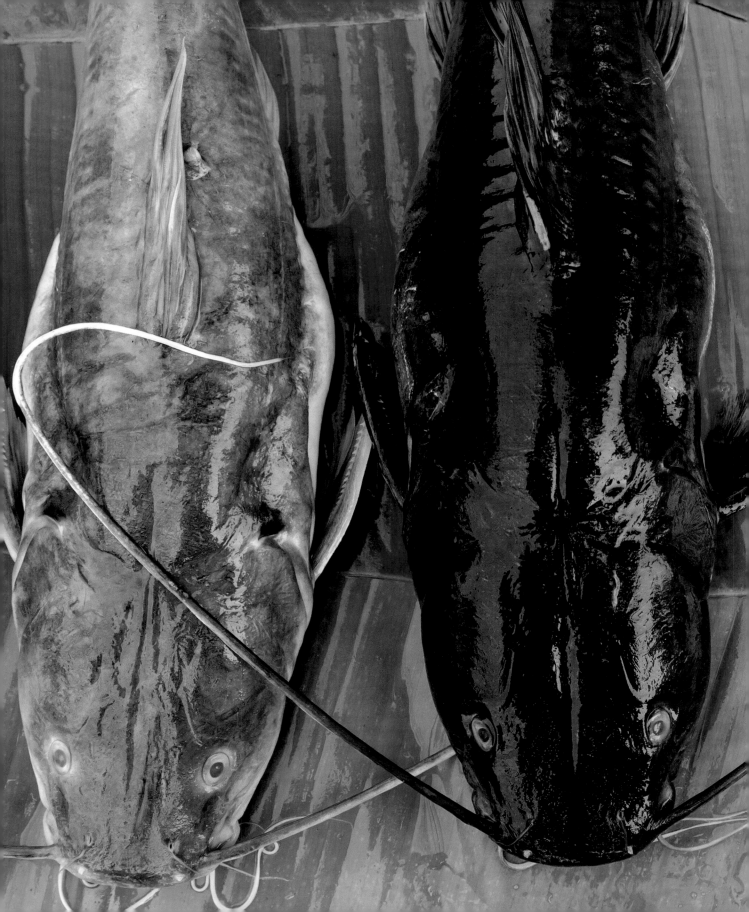

CATFISH

ORIGIN: *Worldwide*

AVAILABILITY: *Year-round*

COMMON FORMS: *Whole; fillets*

STOCK STATUS: *Good, little concern*

SOURCE: *Most retail catfish is farmed; much wild fish is available, though not typically sold in fish shops*

ALTERNATIVES: *striped bass, carp, pike*

FOUND ON EVERY continent outside of Antarctica, catfish have long been a staple of many diets. There are dozens of species throughout the world, ranging from tiny creatures no bigger than 12.5 cm (5 inches) up to the Mekong catfish, which has been caught at sizes over 300 kg (660 lb). In North America, most of the catfish we see are either blue catfish, flathead catfish, or channel catfish. Some wild-caught catfish is available, but the majority of what we eat today is farmed. Though it is raised throughout the United States, more than half of the overall catfish production in North America is located in or around the state of Mississippi.

Catfish is sometimes described as having an insipid or muddy flavour, but I think that folks just have a slight bias against the fish and perceive it as low value, suitable only for the disadvantaged. In fact, there is very little difference between high-quality, fresh catfish and many other white-fleshed fish that represent much poorer choices (basa and tilapia, for example). If you are looking for a mild, inexpensive fillet, it's hard to do better than containment farm–raised American catfish.

CORNMEAL CATFISH

*A few years back, before Hurricane Katrina, I visited New Orleans during Jazz Fest.
(The festival has a much longer official name, but no one uses that.) I stayed with some friends
at a very inexpensive B&B with a real family vibe. It was cheap and cheerful, and it backed right
onto the racetrack that served as the home of the festival. We could hear the music even when we
weren't on site. On top of that, every night the people who ran the B&B offered a communal meal
that you could partake in for a small fee. The father had heard that I was in the fish business, and
asked if I wanted to help fillet some catfish for the night's meal. I love to help with things like that,
so I said sure. I was handed a well-used filleting knife with electric tape on the handle, and pointed
toward about 23 kg (50 lb) of fresh catfish. I had eaten catfish before, usually as a whole fillet
cooked in the pan or blackened, and I asked him how we were going to be preparing it that night.
In that part of New Orleans, I was told, there was only one way to cook catfish: cut into
chunks, rolled in cornmeal, and fried. I would argue that there might be no better way
to enjoy it — especially if you have the sounds of Jazz Fest as your background music.*

300 g medium-grind cornmeal

125 mL (½ cup) all-purpose flour

60 mL (¼ cup) Old Bay seasoning
  or similar

Salt and pepper, to taste

500 mL (2 cups) whole milk or
  buttermilk

2 large eggs

900 g (2 lb) catfish fillets, cut into
  3-cm (1¼-inch) cubes (approx.),
  skin off

Vegetable oil, for frying

Lemon, for squeezing (optional)

In a shallow bowl, combine cornmeal, flour, and seasoning. Taste a small amount; if it tastes a little bland, add some salt and pepper until you are happy. Set aside.

In a medium bowl, whisk together milk and eggs. Add catfish, working in batches if necessary, and mix gently until well coated. Using a slotted spoon, drain catfish, and then roll in the cornmeal mixture until well coated. Remove catfish from cornmeal, shake off any excess, and transfer to a parchment-lined baking sheet.

In a large pot, heat about 3 inches of oil to about 180°C (350°F).

Fry chunks of coated fish, a few at a time, until just golden, 6 to 8 minutes. Serve immediately. Squeeze a bit of lemon on them, if you're a weirdo.

Serves 8 as a hearty appetizer

"Noodling" Catfish

Grabbling, hogging, dogging, stumping — whatever you call it, you're talking about pulling a catfish out of its hole with your bare hands. Practiced mostly in the South and Midwest, noodling catfish is legal in only fifteen states. Some folks say there are environmental concerns, but mostly lawmakers are just worried about the safety of the fishers.

When the rivers warm up to 25°C+ (77°F+) around May/June, female catfish will lay eggs in holes that are then guarded by the males for a period of about two weeks — a little longer than it takes the eggs to hatch. Not only do the males protect the eggs, they "fan" them to prevent silt from building up. The males are very dedicated to this task and will rarely leave their holes, even to eat. These two weeks make up the prime noodling season, one of the more controversial aspects of the catfish fishery. On the one hand, the fish are being caught at their most vulnerable, and if the adult male is caught, the eggs are unlikely to reach maturity, becoming food for other aquatic life and/or getting silted over. The counter-argument is that this method of fishing is extremely localized and has negligible impact on the overall catfish population.

The act of noodling is best done in pairs or small groups. The fisher will wander along the riverbed looking for a likely hole. It's always a bit of a gamble, as the hole might contain a catfish, but it could also be home to a snapping turtle or water moccasin, either of which will cause much greater injury than a catfish. Once a suitable hole is identified, the fisher's assistant will guard the outside edges of the hole to keep the fish from escaping. The fisher will then reach his arm into the hole, gently waving his fingers around like wet noodles until they feel the fish bite down. The gills are then grabbed with the other hand, and the fish is pulled out and brought to the surface with one hand still in its throat. This is where the true danger lies. Though the fish do have teeth — described as feeling like rough sandpaper — and can do some skin damage, it is the surfacing that's trickiest, as the fish can be quite large. In 2017, Nate Williams and Kelly Millsap teamed up to haul in a record 38.5 kg (85 lb) fish in Lake Tawakoni, Texas. By hand. No matter how strong of a swimmer you are, that much live fish on the end of your arm is going to cause some problems.

This method of hand fishing has its roots in Indigenous traditions, and has been passed down from generation to generation of fishers. Today, it still has thousands of practitioners across the United States. But it's not for the faint of heart. The unofficial motto of hand fishing: "If you ain't bleedin', you ain't handfishin'."

─Flatfish─

Fluke, Flounder, and Sole

ORIGIN: *Northeast Pacific, North Atlantic*
AVAILABILITY: *Year-round*
COMMON FORMS: *Whole; fillets*
STOCK STATUS: *Good, little concern*
SOURCE: *Most catch is wild; some farmed European fish available*
ALTERNATIVES: *plaice, turbot*

THERE ARE A number of fish that start out swimming just like any other fish, but then, as they graduate from the larval stage, flop onto their sides, and their eyes migrate to the same side of their heads. These fish all fall into the broad category of flatfish, although scientifically they are all very different. To you and me, though, the difference is mostly semantic. The smaller flatfish all share a similar body structure and flavour: clean, firm, and sweet.

A flounder gets called a "fluke" when a summer flounder flops onto its left side. It stays a flounder when it leans to the right. Either way, it remains essentially the same fish from a culinary perspective.

Many different sole exist in the marketplace, the most desirable of which is referred to as "Dover sole." European Dover sole, or common sole, is quite threatened, so it is best to source farmed fish if buying from Europe. By the way, the chance of your fish actually coming from Dover is basically zero. Most of what gets sold is frozen, fished by the Dutch. On the West Coast of North America, there is also a fish called Dover sole, but it has nothing to do with European sole, and tends to be much smaller. This fish, though not a true sole, is still very delicate and delicious. As well, the West Coast fishery is well managed and considered a good choice by most certifying bodies.

Turbot and plaice are other names that you are likely to see in the small to medium flatfish category. Again, they are almost indistinguishable flavour- and texture-wise from the others on the list.

With all of these choices, gentle handling is your best road to success. Whole flatfish tend to roast very well, with the skin acting as a form of parchment around

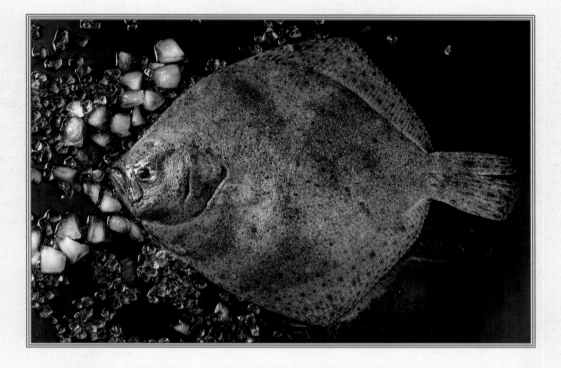

A flounder gets called a "fluke" when a summer flounder flops onto its left side. It stays a flounder when it leans to the right.

the flesh, keeping it moist during the cooking process. Due to escalating prices for high-quality flatfish, many restaurants are offering it in crudo form (raw), which definitely highlights the subtle sweetness of these fish. Trying to pan sear small flatfish fillets will likely lead to a broken mess, unless you are very skilled. If you are feeding a crew and want to serve fillets, a baking sheet, a piece of parchment, and the broiler setting on your oven is your best bet.

WHOLE FLUKE "MEUNIÈRE"

If I'm cooking flatfish, I really prefer to handle it whole. The skin protects the meat, and there is a tiny layer of fat just below the skin that keeps things moist. Very fresh fluke (or sole, turbot, etc.) may have a layer of slime on it, which is normal, even desired. It needs to be rinsed off, though, so make sure you take care of this first. This recipe is a simple classic.

1 whole fluke (1 to 2 kg/2 to 4 lb)

Salt

250 mL (1 cup) clarified butter

250 mL (1 cup) cold butter

1 lemon, sliced into thin rings

1 bunch fresh flat-leaf parsley, roughly chopped

Salt and pepper, to taste

Rub salt all over the skin of the fish, and then let sit on a wire rack in the fridge for an hour or more to dry out.

In a large skillet, on medium-high heat, melt clarified butter. Once the pan is hot, brush the excess salt from the skin of the fish and lay it gently in the pan. Sear fish for 3 to 4 minutes. Flip gently and cook the other side for 3 to 4 minutes. Transfer the cooked fish to a large platter. Set aside.

Wipe the pan clean and add cold butter. Heat until bubbling and just turning brown. Remove the pan from the heat. Add lemon slices and parsley to the browned butter, and stir to combine. Lift the top layer of skin from the fish and discard, and pour the brown butter mixture overtop of the fish.

Allow 500 g (1 lb) per person. A whole fish should yield about 200 to 250 g (7 to 9 oz) filleted as a main.

GURNARD

ORIGIN: *Northeast Atlantic, New Zealand*

AVAILABILITY: *Year-round*

COMMON FORMS: *Whole*

STOCK STATUS: *Good, little concern*

SOURCE: *All catch is wild*

ALTERNATIVES: *catfish*

A PREHISTORIC-LOOKING fish, the gurnard has a large head and tapered body, but what really distinguishes it from the other fish in the sea are its pectoral fins, which open like wings and sweep the ocean floor for food. It's really quite a sight to see the gurnard cruising along the sea bottom with its wings stirring things up.

For years, and to this day, much of the gurnard harvested ends up as bait fish, which is a terrible shame, as it's just as tasty as any other white fish. The yield from each fish is lower than some others, but it tends to be well priced, and it's a fish that we can eat guilt-free. There is little concrete information on gurnard populations, as it hasn't been studied much as a targeted fish, but it seems we aren't doing any great damage to the species, for now. Hopefully, when the gurnard gains in popularity, we can truly get a handle on its habits and future.

As it's such a unique fish, I like to cook and present gurnard whole. Like any white fish, it's flexible. In fillet form, most cooking techniques are appropriate, outside of grilling and smoking, as the flesh of the fish doesn't really stand up too well.

HADDOCK

ORIGIN: *North Atlantic*

AVAILABILITY: *Year-round*

COMMON FORMS: *Fillets*

STOCK STATUS: *Some concern; North American stocks are fairly well-managed, as of recently*

SOURCE: *All catch is wild*

ALTERNATIVES: *cod, snapper*

ONE OF THE staples of the Atlantic fishery, haddock is in the same family as cod, hake, and whiting. It has a fine-grained flesh and is very easy to work with. Various countries are struggling with the management of their stocks. It's a fish that I enjoy, but am starting to pull back from because of its impending and current problems.

In Canada, juvenile haddock stocks (those not yet reproducing) have fluctuated wildly since the early '90s, when they were at historic lows. They are starting to recover, but are still significantly affected by yearly changes in reproduction rates. Due to the fragility of the recovery, Canada and the United States have placed strict controls on Total Allowable Catch (TAC), but the quotas are well below what was allowed into the mid-'90s, and will likely remain low. Look for fisheries that are MSC-certified or certified by another of the independent rating systems. You can be confident with Canadian haddock, though there isn't much of it around.

Haddock has tremendous shelf life, and continues to be edible even after two weeks out of the water. It's certainly better to get the fish in whole form, but it's rare to find it like that. Look for a faint pinkish tone to the flesh and a reasonable amount of moistness. Flesh that is grey/brown and slightly dry will still be edible, but it won't have the same sweetness or be as tender.

⊸HAKE⊸

ORIGIN: *North Atlantic, Pacific North America*
AVAILABILITY: *Year-round*
COMMON FORMS: *Fillets*
STOCK STATUS: *Good, little concern*
SOURCE: *All catch is wild*
ALTERNATIVES: *cod, ling cod*

THE LEAST WELL-KNOWN of the cod family, hake is one of the most important fisheries on the West Coast of North America, and is fished all over the world. Unfortunately, due to its lower perceived value, much of the catch is processed into fish meal and surimi. Fishers can get as little as 10 cents per pound for their fish. Happily, the fishery is, on the whole, well managed. European controls on this fishery, however, are much less stringent than in North America, so be cautious when considering European fish. Look for a certified fishery. Certain environmental groups are concerned not with the level of harvest, but that a perfectly good food fish is being transformed into food for other fish, and this is a needless waste of the resource, and requires excess energy that is essentially wasted in the process.

So let's eat hake! On Prince Edward Island, some people still refer to it as the "Island fish," probably because there was never a big export market for it, so it was the fish eaten by people in the local community, as opposed to the more desirable cod or haddock. When absolutely fresh, hake has a lovely pink tinge to its flesh, with some tiny black spots reminiscent of pepper flakes. The colour will fade as the days go by, but the fish will remain quite delicious, even 10 days after harvest, when kept well. Hake tends to have a less fine grain than cod or haddock, and could be described as meatier. As with all the fish in the family, though, the flavour is quite mild and lends itself to many preparations.

— Classic Deep-Fried Hake — with Ye Olde Tartar Sauce

I don't eat a lot of fried fish, delicious as it is. I just tend to prefer lighter dishes.
Sometimes, though, the stomach wants what the stomach wants.

Vegetable or other high-heat oil,
  for frying
600 g (1.3 lb) hake, filleted and cut into
  4 equal pieces
2 cups (500 mL) all-purpose flour
65 mL (heaping ¼ cup) baking
  powder
325 mL (1⅓ cups) sparkling water or
  light-flavoured beer (classic pilsner
  or lager)
Zest of 1 lemon
10 mL (2 tsp) fresh lemon juice
Ye Olde Tartar Sauce (recipe below)

In a dedicated deep-fryer or deep pot, heat about 5 cm (2 inches) of oil to 160°C (325°F).

Dust each portion of fish with a little flour, and set aside.

In a bowl, whisk together remaining flour, baking powder, sparkling water or beer, and lemon juice and zest until smooth (the mixture should be fluid, but not runny, and stick to a spoon a little bit). Dip each fillet into batter, and carefully lower into the hot oil, trying not to get any hot oil on you. You may need to fry in batches, depending on the size of your pot. Fry each batch of fish for 3 to 4 minutes, until golden. Flip fillets and fry the other side for 2 minutes. Transfer to a wire rack to drain.

Serves 4 as a main course

YE OLDE TARTAR SAUCE

It's time for a guilty pleasure. I won't even force you to make your own mayonnaise.

300 mL (1¼ cups) prepared mayonnaise
75 mL (⅓ cup) chopped gherkin-style pickles (sweet or not, depending on your taste)
50 mL (3 tbsp + 1 tsp) fresh lemon juice
50 mL (3 tbsp + 1 tsp) chopped fresh dill fronds

In a bowl, stir together mayonnaise, chopped pickles, lemon juice, and chopped dill. Serve dolloped next to Deep-Fried Hake (above) or put into ramekins.

Makes 2 cups (500 mL)

JOHN DORY

ORIGIN: *Worldwide, though rarely in North America*
AVAILABILITY: *Year-round*
COMMON FORMS: *Whole; fillets*
STOCK STATUS: *Good, little concern*
SOURCE: *All catch is wild*
ALTERNATIVES: *plaice, turbot*

A STRANGE-LOOKING and fairly lazy fish that doesn't appear much in North American waters, though it has been seen from time to time on eastern Long Island, the John Dory is also commonly referred to as St. Peter's fish, referencing a passage in the Bible (Matthew 17, verse 26). Legend has it that St. Peter caught the fish by hand, leaving his thumbprints on the John Dory, which you can still see on the sides of the fish today. Another story suggests that St. Peter was so startled by the grunting or moaning sound that John Dories sometimes make when landed that he threw the fish back into the sea, leaving his thumbprints. Either way, this is a fish with a past.

John Dories are commonly found off the coast of Europe, Australia, and New Zealand, and are not under any particular population pressure. This is very good news because they happen to be very delicious. When purchased whole, care must be taken to avoid getting stabbed by the very obvious spikes along the top and bottom of the fish. These are best removed with poultry shears, or even a good pair of scissors, before attempting to fillet. The flesh is quite delicate, and I would almost steer people away from cooking it whole, as there is a possibility of drying it out and losing the subtlety of this pricey fish. Fillets will cook very easily, and the resulting head and bones will generate a beautiful stock that can be used to make an accompanying sauce. To me, this is the best use of a John Dory.

Expect to pay a premium for this fish, especially when it originates in Europe or New Zealand. Though it is found worldwide, try to purchase John Dories from countries that have management programs in place for reducing bycatch. It's worth paying a little extra for that reassurance.

JOHN DORY WITH CAPONATA

*Lift four nice fillets from the John Dory, or have your fish shop do it for you.
To fillet the fish, slice firmly into the fish, along the middle, from head to tail. Then work the knife
from the incision, away from the middle, staying along the bone. Keep the skin on, and follow the
recipe below. Serve alongside the caponata, for acidity and freshness. I like the caponata
at room temperature, but it's up to you, if you prefer it warm.*

For the caponata:

2 to 3 small eggplants, peeled and diced

45 mL (3 tbsp) fine salt

250 mL (1 cup) olive oil, divided

1 medium onion, peeled and diced

400 mL (1⅔ cups) canned or bottled
   tomatoes, peeled and seeded

150 mL (⅔ cup) small green olives,
   pitted

2 stalks celery, peeled and diced

250 mL (1 cup) roughly chopped
   celery leaves

150 mL (⅔ cup) dry white wine or
   apple cider vinegar

75 mL (⅓ cup) granulated sugar

Freshly cracked black pepper, to taste

For the John Dory:

4 John Dory fillets, skin-on, patted dry

Salt and pepper

100 mL (6 tbsp + 2 tsp) grapeseed or
   other high-heat oil

1 lemon, cut in half

To make the caponata: Preheat oven to 215°C (420°F).

In a bowl, toss eggplant in salt and 150 mL (⅔ cup) of the oil. Spread evenly over a baking sheet and roast in preheated oven for 30 to 40 minutes, until soft.

Meanwhile, in a medium pot, over medium heat, heat remaining oil. Add onions and cook, stirring occasionally, for 5 to 8 minutes, until onions are softened but not brown. Stir in tomatoes, olives, celery stalks and leaves, wine or vinegar, and sugar. Reduce heat slightly, and simmer for an additional 15 to 20 minutes, until the liquid has somewhat reduced and things soften a bit. Add roasted eggplant, and stir to combine. Simmer for an additional 5 minutes, and then remove from heat. Crack some pepper onto the caponata, if you wish. Will keep in the fridge for up to a week.

To make the John Dory: Dust both sides of the fillets with a generous amount of salt and pepper. In a large pan, over medium-high heat, heat oil. When oil begins to shimmer, gently lay fillets, skin-side down, in the pan and sear for about 5 minutes. Carefully flip fish over, and remove the pan from the heat. The residual heat in the pan will finish cooking the fish. Spoon caponata onto 2 plates and place 2 fillets on each. Serve with lemon garnish.

Serves 2 as a main course

MONKFISH

ORIGIN: *North American East Coast*

AVAILABILITY: *Year-round*

COMMON FORMS: *Fillets, tails*

STOCK STATUS: *Good, some concern, but recent changes in management have improved things*

SOURCE: *All catch is wild*

ALTERNATIVES: *hake, grouper*

BEST KNOWN FOR being one of the ugliest fish that we commonly eat, monkfish is also sometimes referred to as "goosefish" or "anglerfish." The vast majority of the world's supply comes from the East Coast of the U.S. and Canada, and it's now a pretty well-managed fishery. Monkfish was rarely caught as a targeted fishery until the mid-'70s, when landings shot up from under 200,000 pounds annually to just under 10 million pounds by 1980. This kept escalating until the late '90s, when a record haul of over 60 million pounds was recorded. By this time, it was obvious that the fishery needed oversight, as the fish being landed were getting smaller and smaller, and there was conflict with other fisheries. So in the early 2000s, a strong management plan was put into place, and since then stocks have recovered. Landings are much less (under 20 million

pounds), but the overall fishery is much healthier.

Unfortunately, there is concern about the amount of bycatch that is produced as a result of the monkfish harvest. Because of this issue, the fishery is only mildly recommended by some certification bodies, and not recommended at all by others. To me, it is a unique fish with a one-of-a-kind texture that is not easily found in other fish. If you really want to eat monkfish, I don't blame you and I'm not going to stop you, but just keep in mind that there are other, better options out there.

The flesh is sold primarily in the form of the tail or fillets from the tail. You rarely see whole monkfish in shops, and if you did, you wouldn't soon forget. The mouth of these beasts is as wide as the fish is long, and is ringed with menacing teeth. Monkfish will eat prey almost as

large as they are — including birds! They are voracious. The other prized part of the fish is the liver, which can be handled like foie gras and made into a pâté or torchon. Monkfish have one of the best fish livers I have tried. Really delicious. The tail meat is very firm and will stand up to grilling or use in soups, as it doesn't flake apart as readily as other fillets. It's quite easy to work with and has a sweet, satisfying flavour. Some people have referred to monkfish as the "poor man's lobster" due to its flavour and texture, but I think you'd have to be pretty confused to mix up the two. Monkfish is what it is, and that's good enough.

PICKEREL

ORIGIN: *North America freshwater*
AVAILABILITY: *Year-round*
COMMON FORMS: *Whole; fillets*
STOCK STATUS: *Good, little concern*
SOURCE: *Almost all catch is wild*
ALTERNATIVES: *bass, catfish*

THE TERM "PICKEREL" can be a bit confusing. A few species of true pickerel are native to North America and are fish in the pike family. What you typically see sold as pickerel in fish shops is actually walleye, a fish more closely related to perch. The intertwining of the names has its origins in Britain, and despite the constant misnomers, all fish involved are excellent eating and can easily be substituted for one another in any recipe.

The most straightforward variety is the Northern pike — a beautiful lake fish from northern North America that rarely gets sold in shops, mostly due to its awkward Y-shaped bone structure, which doesn't lend itself to easy filleting. If you happen to see one in the shop, I strongly recommend grabbing it, as the flesh is clean and firm, and the whole fish will roast very well.

The true pickerel most commonly seen in the lakes and rivers of North America are the grass pickerel and redfin pickerel. As I mentioned above, they are related to the pike, and are not what you usually see being sold as pickerel. In fact, they are best left to recreational fishing, and are not good choices for the table since they are under pressure in many areas and any concerted commercial fishing efforts would seriously deplete the stocks.

This leaves us with walleye, which sometimes goes by its real name and sometimes goes by pickerel. Either way, it's a great fish — definitely one of the classic lake fishes of North America — and deserves a place at our tables. Towns in Minnesota, Michigan, North and South Dakota, Manitoba, and Saskatchewan have all laid claim to being the "Walleye Capital of the World." As reported in *Northern Wilds* magazine, "some 'capitals'

have large walleye statues to bolster their claim, like Baudette's huge 40-foot-long, 2-ton Willie the Walleye, built in 1959. Minnesota's Garrison, located on Mille Lacs Lake, has had its giant fibreglass walleye since 1980, while the same year at a cost of $10,000, North Dakota's Garrison erected its own 26-foot 820-pound fibreglass Wally the Walleye. A few like Umatilla and Mobridge put their claim on signs or billboards, while other contenders rely on their walleye fishing reputation and/or hold events like the Lake Erie fishing village of Port Clinton's New Year's bash, 'Madness at Midnight Walleye Drop,' when their 20-foot long, 600-pound fibreglass walleye, Captain Wylie, is lowered by crane from a roof in downtown."

Perceptions of Seafood

After having lived and worked in Prince Edward Island, New York, Toronto, and Montreal, I've come to really appreciate each of them in their own way. I don't have a favourite, though it's hard to beat a morning on New London Bay, P.E.I. Each place has such a passion for seafood, and each has its limitations in obtaining it. P.E.I. will never have good shrimp; Montreal and New York have limited access to Mediterranean fish; and Toronto doesn't have a line on the beautiful Massachusetts fish. The U.S. doesn't seem to want to accept European oysters, though those oysters haven't killed anyone in Canada yet. And all of a sudden, I can't get a live American crawfish into Canada, but Greek crawfish? Sure!

Years ago, I fancied opening a big city–style oyster bar in P.E.I., but back then I struggled to get people to pay even a dollar for an oyster in a restaurant. People kept telling me they could "get them for free from my cousin." Eventually, we opened Ship to Shore, but it wasn't "big city" by any means. To me, though, it was a better fit. We served only fish and seafood from the Maritimes. Instead of relying on trucks and airplanes to bring us the best selection, we kept it as simple as possible.

A lot of food has a sense of place, some more than others. To me, seafood is tied to where it comes from or where it has historically been served. New York and Toronto elevate fish; they buy the best and they charge for it. P.E.I. is old school, beautiful, and the salt air can't be replaced. Montreal lies somewhere in between — it's the New Orleans of the North.

Ultimately, the point of seafood is to remind you where you are and just how close you are to the ocean.

PLAICE

ORIGIN: *Northeast and Northwest Atlantic*
AVAILABILITY: *Year-round*
COMMON FORMS: *Whole; fillets, skinless*
STOCK STATUS: *Good, little concern*
SOURCE: *All catch is wild*
ALTERNATIVES: *sole, turbot*

ALONG WITH TURBOT, European plaice is one of the most important groundfish in Northern Europe. It is a slower-growing flatfish, and is not universally well managed. Fisheries in Alaska, Canada, and Iceland, in particular, seem to be stable, and overall are good choices. Plaice tend to be between 3 to 4 kg (6.5 to 9 lb) in size and are mostly sold as skinless fillets. The meat is a beautiful bright white, and is fairly delicate in texture. As with most of the small to medium flatfish, gentle handling is encouraged, though plaice, in particular, is a popular choice for fish and chips in many northern countries.

PORGY

ORIGIN: *Northwest Atlantic as porgy;*
Northeast Atlantic and Mediterranean as bream
AVAILABILITY: *Year-round*
COMMON FORMS: *Whole*
STOCK STATUS: *Good, little concern*
SOURCE: *All catch is wild*
ALTERNATIVES: *snapper, rockfish, bream*

A MUCH-MALIGNED fish that needs to be brought into the forefront, porgy is basically North American sea bream at a very attractive price. Alternately known as "scup" (typically north of New York) or "sheepshead," porgy typically comes from the mid-Atlantic and ranges from 1 to 2 pounds (500 g to 1 kg). Recently, stocks have rebounded from an overall population decline that reached its bottom in the '90s, and we should be celebrating this fact by ensuring that porgy fishers have a strong market to sell into.

Most porgies are caught commercially between June and September. Easy to scale with edible skin, they yield small fillets that are very reminiscent of snapper in taste and texture. But due to their size, porgy is often served whole, which limits its popularity since so many folks prefer a large boneless fillet. This is a shame, as the experience of eating fish off the bone is one that connects us to the fish in a very real way.

PORGY BRANDADE

Brandade is such an easy dish to make, and a mild fish like porgy lends itself to it perfectly. Traditionally made with salt cod, my version swaps in fresh fish, lightly salted, for a result that is moister. Be aware that I do request that you plan ahead a little by salting the fish the night before. It's a small thing to ask.

400 g (14 oz) skinless porgy fillets

15 mL (1 tbsp) salt

2 medium potatoes, peeled and boiled, still warm

1 cup (250 mL) heavy or whipping (35%) cream

5 to 10 mL (1 to 2 tsp) fresh lemon juice

Pinch of ground nutmeg

Salt and pepper, to taste

Lay the fish in a glass baking dish and sprinkle salt all over the fillets, ensuring that all sides get coated. Cover tightly in plastic wrap and refrigerate overnight.

The next day, rinse fish well under cold running water. In a medium pot, cover prepared porgy in about 300 mL (1¼ cups) of water. Cover pot, and set heat to low. Let fish poach/steam for about 10 minutes. Remove from heat and drain. To the same pot, add boiled potatoes, cream, lemon juice, and nutmeg. Return to low heat and, using a potato masher, mash ingredients together. Switch to a loose whisk and start whisking. The mixture should develop a fairly smooth texture, though not perfectly smooth. After about 5 minutes, remove the pan from the heat and taste. Adjust seasoning with salt and pepper, as desired.

Serve warm, with nice toasts.

Serves 4 to 6 as a main course

—Rockfish—

ORIGIN: *Pacific*

AVAILABILITY: *Year-round*

COMMON FORMS: *Fillets*

STOCK STATUS: *Some concern, North American sources are well managed*

SOURCE: *All catch is wild*

ALTERNATIVES: *snapper, ocean perch*

UNTIL THE 1990S, rockfish was considered trash fish, an unwanted bycatch of the various West Coast trawl fisheries. Even recreational anglers weren't much interested in them. But from the mid '80s onward, things began to change. By the early 2000s, there was a huge drop in the rockfish biomass, much of it brought on, surprisingly, by the recreational fishery, which out-caught the commercial fishery for a couple of decades. Stronger management practices have been put into place, and overall the fishery is now strong and stable.

For some reason, some chefs and retailers still hide the true name of the fish, calling it snapper or rock cod instead. This is troubling for a couple of reasons. First, it implies that rockfish is somehow a poorer quality and less tasty fish than others, which is simply not true. And second, it adds to the distrust and perceived deception in the seafood industry, which is harmful to everyone. So let's celebrate a great fish, and a pretty solid management strategy.

There are over 100 types of rockfish in total, and we eat at least 20 of those: China rockfish, tiger rockfish, vermilion rockfish, and more. Some varieties grow in deeper waters, such as the shortraker, and can live up to 200 years. These are not advisable to catch, as they take a long time to mature and to regenerate stocks. Happily, most of what we see in the fish market is caught at shallower depths, and from more stable populations.

PAN-FRIED SKATE

Simple is best with skate. Generally, one wing is enough for two people. The meat pulls off in little strips, and this texture is definitely part of the experience. To some (like our photographer, Rick), the texture can be off-putting, but I love the fact that most every fish offers a unique eating experience. Pair it with a crispy bitter leaf, like Treviso or arugula, to cut the unctuousness of the skate.

1 skate wing, skinless
5 mL (1 tsp) cayenne powder
5 mL (1 tsp) salt
200 mL (¾ cup + 5 tsp) milk
325 mL (1⅓ cups) all-purpose flour
2 tbsp (30 mL) unsalted butter
50 mL (3 tbsp + 1 tsp) grapeseed oil
1 lemon, cut into wedges
Finishing salt, to taste (optional)

Sprinkle half the cayenne and salt onto a plate, and lay the skate wing on top of it, pressing down very gently to ensure seasonings adhere. Dust the other side of the skate with the remaining seasonings. Pour milk into a shallow bowl, and flour in a square pan. Drag the fish first through the milk and then through the flour, ensuring full coverage with both, but especially the flour.

Get a wide sauté pan fairly hot, over medium-high heat. Add butter and oil. When bubbling, swirl the oil in the pan to even it out, and then lay the seasoned skate in the pan. Fry for about 4 minutes. The flesh will turn a light golden brown colour on the higher ridges. No need to brown it too much, as it will get a second crisping. Turn and cook the other side for 4 to 5 minutes. To finish crisping it up, flip the fish again, and cook it for an additional minute on each side. Serve immediately with lemon wedges and finishing salt, if you wish.

Serves 4 as a snack or 2 as a main course with some bitter greens on the side

SNAPPER

ORIGIN: *U.S. Southeast, Gulf of Mexico*
AVAILABILITY: *Year-round*
COMMON FORMS: *Whole; fillets*
STOCK STATUS: *Good, little concern*
SOURCE: *All catch is wild*
ALTERNATIVES: *rockfish, ocean perch, porgy*

ONE OF THE most prized sport fish, snapper is also one of the most delicious — and its value to the commercial fishing industry in the Southeast Atlantic and Gulf of Mexico cannot be overstated. This demand has endangered the red snapper in the past, leading it to perilously low population levels in the 1990s and early 2000s. The recreational fishery has a strong lobby, and much of the overall fishery is now divided between federal and state waters. Meanwhile, a lot of fish are falling through the cracks. Through strong conservation efforts mostly aimed at reducing bag limits and season lengths, the recovery of the snapper population is in sight. It is a fish that can — and should — be enjoyed relatively guilt-free.

Sadly, much of what is sold as red snapper is probably not. Due to its relative scarcity and seasonality, there is a huge temptation for chefs and retailers to misrepresent what they are selling. It's best to be cautious when offered red snapper. Look for whole fish, or at least skin-on fillets. And it won't be cheap. If it seems like too good of a deal, it probably is.

There are, however, several other good snapper choices — yellowtail, B-liner, vermilion, and mingo — which are all varieties that you may see in the fish market. Due to their diminished popularity, the pressure on these populations is much reduced, so you can feel safe purchasing them as long as they are fished in the United States.

B-liner or vermilion snappers have a similar appearance to red snappers, and will be sold as such from time to time, though they tend to be smaller. It seems that the name B-liner comes from the fact that they are considered to be below the red snapper, which are considered A-line. Don't be discouraged by this — these fish are every bit as tasty as red snapper.

Red Snapper Hot and Sour Soup

*The head and bones of this fish make beautiful stock,
and buying the fish whole ensures that you are truly getting red snapper.*

1 whole red snapper (2 to 3 kg/4 to 6.6 lb), scaled and gutted

4 L (16 cups) water

1 onion, quartered

2 stalks celery, roughly chopped

50 mL (3 tbsp + 1 tsp) vegetable or other high-heat oil

3 shallots, finely chopped

5 cloves garlic, sliced

200 mL (¾ cup + 5 tsp) finely chopped lemongrass

40 mL (2 tbsp + 2 tsp) tamarind paste

Pinch of ground turmeric

30 mL (2 tbsp) cane sugar

30 mL (2 tbsp) chili paste (sambal oelek or similar) or 5 long red chilies (cayenne, ripe jalapeño), minced with seeds

30 mL (2 tbsp) fish sauce

Zest and juice of 3 limes

Fillet the snapper, leaving the skin on, reserving the head and bones for stock. Cut fillets into four equal portions and set aside.

In a large pot, combine water, reserved fish head and bones, onion, and celery. Bring to a rapid boil over high heat, then reduce heat to medium-low, and simmer for about 30 minutes, skimming off the foam occasionally. Using a fine-mesh sieve, strain the stock and set aside; discard solids. (You should end up with approximately 600 to 700 mL/2½ to 3 cups fish stock. If you don't end up with quite enough, add some canned clam stock, other fish stock, or even a splash of chicken stock — it's a savoury enough soup that a hint of poultry won't kill it.)

In a medium pot, over low heat, combine oil, shallots, garlic, lemon grass, tamarind, and turmeric. Sauté for about 10 minutes, until shallots and garlic are softened and turning translucent. Add strained fish stock, sugar, chili paste, fish sauce, and lime zest and juice, and bring to a low boil. Taste and adjust heat, sweetness, and sourness, if you like, by adding lime, sugar, and/or chili paste. Remove from heat and gently place snapper fillets into broth (they will cook from the residual heat). Let sit for 5 to 6 minutes.

Divide fish and broth evenly among serving bowls. Garnish with chopped coriander and basil.

Serves 4

TILAPIA

ORIGIN: *Asia, Southeast Asia, Central America, United States*
AVAILABILITY: *Year-round*
COMMON FORMS: *Fillets*
STOCK STATUS: *Good, little concern, though best to buy North or Central American; potential environmental and human rights issues with other sources*
SOURCE: *All catch is cultivated*
ALTERNATIVES: *catfish, branzino, bream, striped bass*

WITH ORIGINS IN Africa and the Middle East, tilapia has now spread into many other temperate and warm regions of the world. References to the fish can be seen in Egyptian hieroglyphs, and it's suspected that tilapia is the fish that is referenced in the Biblical story of the miracle of the loaves and fishes. Some artisanal fishing of tilapia still occurs in Africa, but almost everything that is commercially harvested is farmed.

Tilapia is one of the more adaptable fish, and it can grow in a wide variety of salinity, though it's pickier about temperature, with very little survival in water temperatures below 7°C (44.5°F). This has led to its introduction to many areas where it is considered invasive. American-farmed tilapia is typically a good if insipid choice that is easy to prepare. Most worldwide production, though, is from China, as tilapia's main attraction is its low price, since it thrives on lower-cost soy and grain meal. Chinese fish farms have spotty environmental and human rights records, so it is difficult to recommend fish from this region. If you're looking at tilapia in the fish market, make sure it's from North or Central America.

As it is sold almost exclusively in fillet form, tilapia is easy to prepare, with a very mild flavour, comparable to catfish or seabass. Simple pan-searing or frying work well; grilling not so much. Tilapia is not a fish that I would recommend for crudo or ceviche.

—TROUT—

ORIGIN: *Worldwide*
AVAILABILITY: *Year-round*
COMMON FORMS: *Whole; fillets*
STOCK STATUS: *Good, little concern*
SOURCE: *Most trout are farmed; small amount of wild lake trout available*
ALTERNATIVES: *char, salmon*

OF ALL THE pink fish, I'm always disappointed that trout has yielded the throne to salmon. I couldn't possibly love trout any more, but sadly, my love is not universally shared.

Brook, rainbow, brown, and the many other trouts all share the same flexibility: They can be roasted whole, pan-seared, smoked, or cured. The eggs are delicious and beautiful — golden to red, with a distinct pop. There is a small percentage of wild trout in the market, though the vast majority is farmed, which shouldn't stop anyone from purchasing it. In general, North American trout farms are well run,

efficient operations. The fish are every bit as tasty as what you find in the wild, and they're consistently available.

Most trout are freshwater, with the exception of steelhead trout, which have seen salt water for part of their life. For inland city dwellers, this gives them another distinct advantage: They can be a local product with the commensurate boost in freshness. As well, your trout could be coming from your neighbours, and you will be contributing to the virtuous circle of keeping money in your community.

ROASTED WHOLE TROUT

The secret to cooking a whole medium to large fish is to first get a nice char or crisp on the skin, and then to finish the fish at a lower, indirect heat. This gives you texture and smoke on the skin, melts the fat between the skin and the flesh, and generally allows for more control.

Whether you're using a grill and charcoal, propane, or a pan on a stove to get the fish started, it makes very little difference. I prefer wood/charcoal, but you can get great results from a hot pan as well. Be warned: there will be smoke! So it's best to start the fish outdoors if at all possible.

Have your fishmonger gut the fish for you, or do it yourself, but make sure the cavity of the fish is well cleaned and rinsed before you start. There may be a bit of slime on the outside of the fish, which is completely normal and even beneficial. But the slime should be rinsed off as best you can before cooking. Once the fish is cleaned and rinsed, pat it dry with some paper towels. Oil it liberally inside and out with a high-heat oil, such as canola, grapeseed, or avocado. Sprinkle salt and pepper everywhere on the fish. Some folks stuff the fish with herbs and lemon, but I find that effort sort of pointless, as almost no flavour will be imparted from these trappings. Put those things in a sauce to be served on the side.

Once the fish is oiled and salted, get your grill or pan quite hot — not maximum heat, but at 70 to 80 percent. Lay the fish onto the heat, and let it cook, undisturbed, for 3 to 4 minutes. The smoke produced is fine, and desired. Using a spatula or two, gently flip the fish over and grill the other side for 3 to 4 minutes, until the skin is crispy (the flesh will still have a mostly bright tone and will turn opaque as it cooks in the oven). Transfer the fish to a parchment-lined baking sheet and bake in a preheated 230°C (450°F) oven for 10 to 15 minutes, depending on the size of the fish. For 1 kg (2 lb) and under, 10 minutes should be fine; for 1.5 to 2 kg (3 to 4 lb), go a bit longer. If you have a trout bigger than that, congratulations! Go a couple of more minutes, but not too many. The fish should be slightly undercooked when you pull it from the oven. Let it rest, somewhere warmish, for another 5 minutes or so (it will finish cooking from the residual heat).

Just before serving, pour a little melted butter or olive oil overtop of the whole thing. The fat can have other flavourings, such as lemon zest or juice, capers, cracked black pepper, tarragon, or thyme, which is the best way to infuse flavours into the meal.

A 1 kg (2 lb) trout will serve 2 to 3 folks, maybe 4 if you have lots of side dishes. A 1.5 to 2 kg (3 to 4 lb) fish will look after 4 to 6 people.

Setting Up a Trout Pond in Queens, New York

Hugue was as sick as I'd ever seen him. This wasn't good, as we were getting ready to open in just two days. Of more immediate concern, however, were the 70 live trout that were landing the next morning in our cobbled-together trout pond.

Let me back up a bit. A couple friends of mine, Hugue Dufour and Sarah Obraitis, were opening their third — and most complicated — restaurant, M. Wells Steakhouse, in what could generously be described as a nondescript neighbourhood, Long Island City, Queens. Everyone was very nervous, as it was a very expensive endeavour, and it was the kind of place that people would need to make an effort to reach. I had been helping out Hugue and Sarah for the past few weeks to get them over the hurdle of finally opening their doors. In fact, I'd been living at the restaurant in a small airstream-style trailer parked in a large back room. I'd been literally camping in a restaurant in the middle of Queens. The things you do for friends.

Though it was being called a steakhouse, Hugue wanted a large seafood component to the menu, and part of that was an Alsatian dish called *truite au bleu*, or blue trout. For this dish, you need absolutely fresh fish with all of their slime intact. By fresh, I mean killed only minutes before being dropped in the pot. It has to do with a chemical reaction between the slime and a vinegar bath that the fish gets immersed in just before cooking. The skin of the fish turns bright blue and stays that way. It's a beautiful dish — something Hugue had dreamed about putting on a menu. The problem was, where do you find live trout in New York City? And how do you keep them alive until the moment of preparation?

> *I'd been literally camping in a restaurant in the middle of Queens. The things you do for friends.*

Hugue had solved the second part of the problem. On one part of the kitchen line, he had built a concrete well that was theoretically big enough for 60 to 70 live trout. One thing he hadn't considered, though, was oxygenating and filtering the water. I scoured Queens in the weeks before opening to find suitable pumps, hoses, and filters for an aquarium of this size and type. All of this was, of course, hampered by the fact that I barely knew the city, and we had many other fires to put out — typical of any restaurant opening. Nonetheless, I figured we had a suitable set-up.

A week earlier we'd visited a cool trout research facility that mostly involved stocking New York State rivers and lakes with trout on an annual basis. They had the fish in sufficient numbers, they had the custom delivery vehicle, and most importantly, they were willing to bring the fish into the city in relatively small quantities for a reasonable price! (We also made a deal for their extra eggs — they made fantastic trout caviar.) Everything was in place for our big delivery, when just the day before, Hugue got sick. We were all exhausted, nervous, and at our limits, and normally we would have delayed the trout delivery, but it was important to Hugue to have them on the menu opening weekend.

The problem was, where do you find live trout in New York City? And how do you keep them alive until the moment of preparation?

So, at around 7 a.m. on the designated morning, about four or five cooks and I met at the restaurant. The special truck pulled up shortly after, and we began gently transferring the trout, in buckets, into the restaurant trout tank. Or at least we tried. Trout love to jump, and I'm sure we ended up with about a third of them hitting the floor before we got the hang of it. Forty-five minutes later it was done. The fish were in the tank, and the truck was gone. Everything seemed to be working.

By the end of the day, though, some of the fish started turning upside down — still alive, but struggling. I had wondered about water temperature earlier, but with all of the lights on at full-strength, we definitely had a problem. Quickly, I started dumping buckets of ice cubes into the tank, got it stabilized, and all was back to normal. Refrigeration was the next fix, but we were on our way.

—TURBOT—

ORIGIN: *Northwest Atlantic, Canada, and Greenland*
AVAILABILITY: *Year-round*
COMMON FORMS: *Whole; fillets*
STOCK STATUS: *Good, little concern*
SOURCE: *All catch is wild*
ALTERNATIVES: *plaice, fluke, flounder*

THE CLOSEST THAT Canada has come to war with a European country in recent years occurred in 1995 — over fish. To be exact, it was the turbot, which most of us haven't even tried, much less developed a passion worth going to war over. Passions in Newfoundland, however, were running extremely high — especially coming so soon after the collapse of the cod fishery in 1992. Foreign vessels were blamed for overfishing of the cod, and the Canadian government wasn't about to let the same thing happen to turbot — the main fishery left to Newfoundlanders. The Canadian Navy fired warning shots, boarded, and seized a Spanish trawler, accusing it of using illegal nets and having unreported cargo. Brian Tobin, then Canada's Fisheries Minister, was in New York at a global conference. Over Spain's objections, he displayed the alleged net used and some examples of the fish found on board. Holding up a fish smaller than his hand, he proclaimed: "We are down to the last, lonely, unloved, unattractive little turbot, clinging by its fingernails to the Grand Banks of Newfoundland, saying 'Someone, reach out and save me in this eleventh hour as I'm about to go down to extinction.'" The ploy worked, the Spanish backed down, and turbot management was strengthened.

Efforts to maintain the fishery since then have been successful, as evidenced by the continued strength of turbot landings reported in Newfoundland. Canadian consumers, on the other hand, have yet to embrace it as a desired fish. Asian markets, primarily Vietnam, Hong Kong, Japan, and China, continue to make up the majority of turbot sales from Canadian waters.

Also known as Greenland halibut, the turbot is essentially a smaller version of the Atlantic halibut and, as such, it's surprising that we don't see more of it in local fish markets. A well-managed, mild, firm whitefish that is extremely versatile, turbot should not be ignored when shopping for fish.

—WHITEFISH—

ORIGIN: *North America freshwater*
AVAILABILITY: *Year-round*
COMMON FORMS: *Whole; fillets*
STOCK STATUS: *Good, management is strong, though availability is decreasing*
SOURCE: *All catch is wild*
ALTERNATIVES: *pickerel, catfish, striped bass*

LONG A STAPLE of the border states and provinces, whitefish has declined in overall abundance. Once a plentiful and cheap fish, whitefish was one of the main sources for gefilte fish when European Jews first came to North America. It was also used to produce a beautiful smoked product, which came in very handy during the long winters. I'm a huge fan of whitefish caviar: The tiny golden eggs, with their mild fishiness and firm pop, are one of the things I look forward to most each fall. Whitefish caviar is criminally underpriced and underappreciated.

In general, whitefish can be handled like any other medium, firm-fleshed fish. It does tend to be on the fattier end of the scale, which is why it lends itself to better smoking results. It is also a great fish for chowder and soup. Its shelf life is somewhat shorter than other less fatty fish, so it should be dealt with quickly after purchase. The flesh will have a nice shine when fresh, but will turn somewhat yellow within a few days, and should be avoided at that point. It should keep for up to three days, refrigerated.

WOLFFISH

ORIGIN: *Northeast Atlantic*

AVAILABILITY: *Year-round*

COMMON FORMS: *Fillets*

STOCK STATUS: *Unclear, some concern,
but not enough information currently available*

SOURCE: *All catch is wild*

ALTERNATIVES: *cod, monkfish*

ONE OF THE ugliest fishes to ever grace a plate, the Atlantic wolffish is nonetheless a delicious fish, reminiscent of the most tender and fluffy cod. In fact, it has been prized for fish and chips in the United Kingdom for many years. Wolffish live at great depth, and have a form of antifreeze in their bodies that allows them to survive even the coldest conditions. They sport a fearsome set of teeth (many sets in fact), and have an eel-like body structure.

To this day, very little is known about their overall population health, and there is great concern that they are particularly susceptible to habitat destruction via aggressive trawling for other species. As well, they tend to appear as bycatch, which also puts pressure on their numbers. I certainly recommend trying wolffish, if given the opportunity, but be aware that it is potentially a fish that will disappear from menus altogether over the next few years.

—WRECKFISH—

ORIGIN: *United States mid-Atlantic,*
New Zealand, Australia

AVAILABILITY: *Year-round*

COMMON FORMS: *Fillets*

STOCK STATUS: *Good, little concern*

SOURCE: *All catch is wild*

ALTERNATIVES: *grouper, tilefish*

FEWER THAN TEN boats in the United States have commercial wreckfish licenses, and the total catch for the year is less than 2 million pounds. The management of the fishery is very strict, so if you ever happen to spot it at a fish market or on a restaurant menu, consider yourself lucky. Do not pass up the chance to nab a piece of this beautiful fish (a piece is all you will likely get, as they are typically 27 to 32 kg/60 to 70 lb and can grow to up to 90 kg/200 lb), reminiscent of grouper or very large sea bass.

Named for their habit of hiding out in caves or shipwrecks, wreckfish are a deep-water and slow-growing fish. They are caught almost exclusively off an area referred to as the Charleston Bump, which is well offshore from the South Carolina/Georgia border, just before the ocean floor drops off sharply. The slope of the Bump drives the Gulf current and provides nutrients for many fish, as well as caves for the wreckfish. It is a unique area that supports a unique fishery. Fishers can fish for days with very little room for error at extreme depths (366+ metres/1200+ feet) to pull in a reasonable catch.

In New Zealand, there is a version of wreckfish, sometimes referred to as "hapuku" or "hapuka," which is a well managed and relatively important fishery. There is some export of this fish to North America, and it is worth looking for.

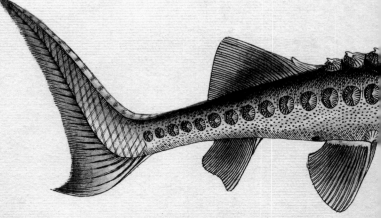

—LARGE FISH—

I cover many beloved fish in this section, some of which have become very problematic from a conservation standpoint. Larger fish can also contain higher concentrations of heavy metals, such as mercury, which is also a concern for some folks. When carefully chosen, however, big fish can still have a big future in our food supply.

Of course, due to their size you will rarely be buying a whole fish — though I've cooked some 7 to 9 kg (15 to 20 lb) groupers in my day, which were absolutely gorgeous and memorable. Fish fillets sometimes present unique challenges for consumers, as clues to freshness, like gill colour and eye shininess, are absent. But, overall, you shouldn't approach larger fish any differently than you would smaller ones. If fact, they can often be easier to cook, as they tend to have firmer flesh with large flakes and a more forgiving nature. The meat-to-bone ratio is much higher with these fish, of course, and they can make for a better

choice for anyone who tends to be squeamish of fish, as the flesh from big fish more closely resembles traditional meat.

We need to be cautious with some of our big-fish decisions, but for well-managed species there is no need to shy away from these wonderful creatures. As fish get larger, they do sometimes become more expensive, but if you opt for a 150 to 175 g (5 to 6 oz) piece, you'll find them within budget. It's easier for the fish cutter to sell you a bigger piece, for sure, but be firm about your request, and they'll honour it.

Behold the beauty of some wonderful monsters of the deep!

For advice on handling and storage, see page 277.

BIGEYE & YELLOWFIN TUNA

ORIGIN: *United States mid-Atlantic,*
New Zealand, Australia
AVAILABILITY: *Year-round*
COMMON FORMS: *Fillets*
STOCK STATUS: *North American fish, well-caught, is of*
low concern; outside of North America, it is harder to justify purchasing
SOURCE: *All catch is wild*
ALTERNATIVES: *grouper, tilefish*

BIGEYE TUNA AND yellowfin tuna are sometimes used almost interchangeably, as they both have deep red flesh (though yellowfin is a bit lighter in colour) and a "meaty" flavour, reminiscent of bluefin tuna. Both can be referred to as "ahi tuna," as there is no real definition of that phrase outside of Hawaii.

With tuna in general, and these larger tunas in particular, both good and bad sourcing options exist. All tuna are wild caught. From time to time, you'll see a farm-raised or -ranched fish, but these are just juvenile wild-caught fish raised in captivity, and aren't any better than properly caught wild adult fish. To be sure that you are eating yellowfin and bigeye

that are responsibly caught, look for the following fishing methods: handline, troll and pole, harpoon, greenstick, and purse seine (unassociated). The "unassociated" refers to the use — or absence — of so-called fish aggregating devices (FAD). FADs are "fish magnets" that are rapidly becoming the go-to choice for careless fishing boats looking to collect the most fish with the least effort. While this is certainly an admirable goal on its own, FADs tend to pick up many other species, and much of this bycatch, which can contain all sorts of endangered species, is thrown away. FAD fishing is one of the most significant recent fishing advances, and one of the most controversial. Another typical method of catching tuna is longlining, which sounds very close to handlining, but involves lines sometimes over 100 kilometres (62 miles) long with thousands of hooks catching all kinds of wildlife.

Both bigeye and yellowfin tuna are found worldwide in warmer waters, from southern Nova Scotia all the way to the Indian Ocean. Most of the well-caught fish you'll find in restaurants and stores will be from North America. It's difficult to truly certify other fisheries. These tunas can be somewhat addictive, but I think we should allow ourselves the odd treat of bigeye or yellowfin, as long as we are being careful about its origin.

These fish typically exceed 90 kg (200 lb), so you are only ever going to see small pieces in the display case. The meat has a tendency to oxidize, meaning it will turn from a fresh ruby red to a muddled brown as it ages. The terms "sushi grade" or "sashimi grade" mean absolutely nothing, except that the fishmonger has decided that they are of sufficient freshness to be eaten as is. It is strictly a matter of how confident you are in your retailer. Large tunas are one of the very few fish that can safely be eaten raw without previously freezing the flesh. Look for well-wrapped, bright red meat, and make sure you keep it wrapped in your fridge.

Large tunas are one of the very few fish that can safely be eaten raw without previously freezing the flesh.

Black Cod

ORIGIN: *North American Pacific*

AVAILABILITY: *Year-round*

COMMON FORMS: *Whole; fillets*

STOCK STATUS: *Strong management*

SOURCE: *Most of the catch is wild; small amounts of farmed fish available*

ALTERNATIVES: *ling cod, sturgeon*

For some reason, we still export over 70 percent of the sablefish (the official name of black cod) caught annually in North American waters to Japan. To me, this is a tragic loss. I'm sure it's being enjoyed by appreciative customers in Japan, but I wish North Americans would realize that black cod is both delicious and easy to prepare. It's also a well-managed fishery that's essentially unique to our waters.

If you have seen black cod, it's likely been on a menu, miso-glazed or some such preparation. The restaurant Nobu popularized this dish in the '90s, and it has spread with the ferocity of molten chocolate cakes (another recipe clichéd by overuse). It's delicious, to be sure, but sablefish has so many possible uses that it would be a shame to limit yourself to just this one dish. Wrap it in collard greens and steam it in a savoury broth, or sear it to the point of caramelization. Black cod can stand up to whatever you throw at it and still be just as tasty as ever.

-BLUEFIN TUNA-

ORIGIN: *Worldwide*

AVAILABILITY: *Year-round*

COMMON FORMS: *Fillets*

STOCK STATUS: *To be avoided; while there are small pockets of well-caught and -managed fish, the global biomass is severely threatened, and the continued presence on especially high-end menus has led to many unscrupulous practices*

SOURCE: *All catch is wild; small amounts of farmed fish available*

ALTERNATIVES: *yellowfin tuna, bigeye tuna, albacore, wahoo (ono)*

WHILE WORLDWIDE CONSENSUS has led us to the conclusion that strong limits need to be placed on the bluefin fishery, and the International Commission for the Conservation of Atlantic Tunas (ICCAT) has set progressively lower quotas on catches, the fish remains critically endangered due to both overfishing in the late 1990s and early 2000s, and more significantly, ongoing illegal fishing. In 2007, when the ICCAT worldwide quota was set at about 30,000 tons, the estimated illegal catch was about the same, in effect doubling the bluefin tuna caught. Even now, with the ICCAT quota at just 14,000 tons, illegal fishing more than doubles the overall catch. A French- and U.S.-led effort to stop all sales of bluefin tuna in 2010 was quashed by Japanese protest and European abstention. A full ban is probably the only way to allow stocks to recover, as the temptation to fish this extremely valuable species is too great. Another hidden danger of illegal fishing is the number of undersized and juvenile fish being captured. In every haul of illegal fish that is seized, undersized fish are present. This is even more damaging to the chances of population recovery than mere overfishing.

There is no way that I can comfortably recommend the purchase and consumption of bluefin tuna. Despite the few controlled fisheries available, the continued trade in this fish will hasten its demise. It is almost impossible to prove that the piece of tuna you're looking at isn't from a fish that was over quota or off the books.

Is There Such a Thing as "Sushi Grade" Fish?

If you've spent some time in fish shops, you've likely come across a sign that says "sushi grade." It's possible that you've even asked the question, "Is this fish okay for sashimi? Is it sushi grade?" As a species, we eat a fair amount of raw fish, which is a little odd considering how little raw meat we eat. Sure, we might enjoy the occasional beef tartare, but that's about it. The thing is, eating raw fish is not inherently better than eating any other protein raw, especially when you consider all of the potential hazards.

There are only two types of finfish that the FDA considers sufficiently low risk to be eaten raw: any of the bigger tunas (yellowtail, bigeye, bluefin) and any saltwater aquaculture fish that's been fed a pellet-only diet. This doesn't mean that everything else should be avoided the next time you're thinking crudo, only that there are risks involved. It's also important to note that you're not necessarily safer eating raw fish at a restaurant than you are at home. Yes, they may have more knowledge than you about food safety, but that doesn't necessarily mean that they've eliminated all hazards. Again, it is all about your tolerance for risk.

Most fish, when frozen for a week at -20°C (-4°F) or below, or a day at -35°C (-31°F) or below, will be clear of parasites. If the fish is especially thick, these times may need to be extended. Your household fridge is unlikely to meet the -35°C (-31°F) mark, though it may get down to -20°C (-4°F). If you plan to freeze fish at home, it's worth checking your freezer with an accurate thermometer. Sushi restaurants will likely be selling fish from a dedicated raw fish supplier whose freezers meet these requirements.

Really, the only federal requirements for declaring a fish "safe" for raw consumption is whether it was frozen correctly or fits into the category of low-risk fish. "Sushi grade," then, is a meaningless label. But there are ways to shop for fish that is lower risk. Most scallops, for example, have a very low pathogen risk. We eat oysters and clams raw all the time. Lobsters and shrimp can carry listeria, so they should probably be avoided raw. As far as unfrozen finfish goes, definitely stay away from freshwater fish — they are more likely to contain parasites, such as tapeworms. Ocean fish are the way to go here.

Really, the only federal requirements for declaring a fish "safe" for raw consumption is whether it was frozen correctly or fits into the category of low-risk fish.

If I'm preparing a crudo or ceviche, I prefer to buy whole fish, gutted. It's important to keep the raw fish as cold as possible, and to rinse it well just before filleting (see page 282) and removing the gills and fins. Make sure that your work area is sanitized and dry. Working quickly, lift the fillets off the bone, remove and discard the skin, rinse fillets under cold water, and place in a clean dish. Once all fillets are cleaned, re-sanitize your work station and, using paper towel or a clean kitchen towel, dry the fillets well.

Tightly cover fillets in plastic wrap and refrigerate if not serving right away (do not leave the fillets in the fridge for more than a day). Carefully examine each fillet under very bright light. If you see the odd worm or rogue thing in the flesh, remove it. Using a clean knife and clean, dry hands, cut fillets into thick pieces. Inspect the pieces as you plate them and remove anything that doesn't look like a normal part of the flesh.

If you buy whole fish from a trusted store and handle it well, you should be fine. Millions of people have safely eaten raw fish, and you can, too.

—COBIA—

ORIGIN: *Southeast United States, Gulf of Mexico, Panama, China, Southeast Asia*

AVAILABILITY: *Year-round*

COMMON FORMS: *Fillets*

STOCK STATUS: *Good, little concern*

SOURCE: *Most of the catch is farmed*

ALTERNATIVES: *kingfish, swordfish, mahi-mahi*

ANYONE WHO HAS fished for cobia along the Gulf coast knows the beauty of this fish. They are sharklike in appearance, and the meat is firm and flavourful, sort of a cross between swordfish and albacore. As lovely as it is, however, cobia has never been more than a recreational fish, as they tend to live solitary lives and are not easy to catch in great numbers. Happily, they are good candidates for aquaculture, and studies are underway to expand the cobia farming industry.

When it comes to many of the larger, firm-fleshed fish, such as mahi and swordfish, it's very important to remove the bloodline — a blood-rich muscle that runs along the length of the fish — because it has a slightly stronger (fishy) flavour that most people like to avoid.

To remove the bloodline, insert the tip of your knife about 1 cm (½ inch) away from the bloodline and carefully cut out the entire red band of flesh in a V-shape. To remove larger bloodlines, you may have to cut the fillet into two portions.

Cobia are sold either whole gutted with the head removed or in fillet form. One of the concerns with a fish like cobia is its levels of mercury. Because the open ocean farm is so far removed from any heavy metal sources, this potential drawback has been eliminated. Cobia tends to be on the pricier side, but because of its many pluses, it is a fish that I would strongly recommend. It's fantastic in a crudo or grilled, thanks to its slightly fattier nature and firmness.

GROUPER

ORIGIN: *Worldwide, though Southeast United States and Gulf of Mexico fish is closest to what we consider "grouper"*

AVAILABILITY: *Year-round*

COMMON FORMS: *Whole; fillets*

STOCK STATUS: *Mostly well managed in United States, especially red, gag, and black grouper*

SOURCE: *All catch is wild*

ALTERNATIVES: *tilefish, monkfish*

THE GROUPER FAMILY ranges widely in size and population. Some examples, such as the goliath grouper, can reach over 363 kg (800 lb). They are not inherently dangerous to humans, even at their largest, as they don't have a strong bite, though many fishers claim that grouper are negatively impacting other fisheries. Many fishers also feel that grouper populations have rebounded to the point that they should be allowed to fish them again. Scientists refute both claims and keep strict controls on all of the Southern U.S. grouper populations.

Certain U.S. groupers are well managed and make good choices, including red, gag, and black groupers. I would steer away from any other varieties, and any grouper at all that is not fished in the United States.

Buying a whole grouper is a somewhat disappointing experience, as after filleting the fish you are left with less than half of what you purchased. Their heads make up a significant percentage of their body weight, and the actual yield is quite small compared to most other fish. When buying a whole fish, budget for about 500 g (1 lb) of whole weight per person, as this will yield about 175 g (6 oz) of fillet. The flesh of all groupers is very firm with large flakes. It's perfect for grilling, chowders, and frying, as it can stand up to these cooking methods better than more delicate fish. It's not a particularly fatty fish, though, so take care when grilling to remove it just a little before you think you should, and let the residual heat finish the cooking. If you need to, pop it into the oven to finish the cooking if you feel it's underdone. It's easier to add a little more heat than it is to add moisture back into an overcooked piece of grouper.

HALIBUT

ORIGIN: *Pacific North;*
American Northwest; Northeast Atlantic
AVAILABILITY: *Year-round*
COMMON FORMS: *Fillets*
STOCK STATUS: *Good, little concern, though a*
relatively large amount is discarded as bycatch from
other fisheries, which is a source of worry
SOURCE: *Almost all catch is wild;*
small amounts of farmed fish recently available
ALTERNATIVES: *turbot, fluke*

HALIBUT IS TRADITIONALLY one of the most valuable groundfish fisheries in North America, especially since the decline of the Atlantic cod stocks. Most halibut sold in stores and restaurants is Pacific halibut, which is a distinct species from Atlantic halibut. In fact, there is no targeted American Atlantic halibut fishery at the moment. In Canada, there is still a small Atlantic quota, which is divided among four provinces, but it represents less than 5 percent of total North American halibut landings.

Due to the importance placed on the continued health of the Pacific halibut fishery, a number of controls have been put into place, including onboard monitoring cameras, strict reporting of catch and discards, and dockside monitoring of landings. There is still some conflict, especially in Alaska, between larger boats, which account for the majority of the West Coast bycatch, and smaller "family" boats, which are the actual halibut quota holders. The big boats are targeting other species, such as pollock, but end up with halibut in their large nets. Some of this can be kept, but much has to be thrown overboard. Theoretically, this is supposed to reduce the eventual bycatch, as it is reported as a percentage of their overall catch and is capped. Unfortunately, when you are talking about hundreds of millions of pounds of targeted allowable fish, and a 1 percent allowed bycatch, that means there are still millions of pounds of halibut being thrown away each year. This is reducing the quotas for smaller

Inside Halibut PEI, an on-land indoor halibut fish farm on P.E.I.

halibut fishers. It is a tough situation with no immediate resolution.

For consumers, however, the halibut picture remains bright. As long as you are buying Pacific halibut or certified Canadian Atlantic halibut, you are safe. Expect to pay a lot for it, though. All of these controls and quotas translate into increased landed costs for this prized fish. The days of halibut fish and chips are mostly gone, except for a few well-heeled cities. There are some halibut aquaculture operations, and they are showing promise for maintaining a small amount of Atlantic halibut, but are also fairly expensive, and the fish produced tend to be smaller and more akin to sole or plaice. They are still delicious, but not what you would expect from traditional halibut.

An All-You-Can-Eat Halibut Buffet, If You're a Killer Whale

Back in the 1950s, when longline fishing became more common, isolated reports began to surface of predator fish, mostly killer and sperm whales, following boats to feast on the fish caught on their lines. Until the '90s, though, these incidents weren't widespread enough to be considered serious. Now, however, it's a global problem. In North America, from British Columbia to the Bering Strait, reports of miles-long catches being decimated — the whales sometimes leaving "nothing but lips" — are beginning to attract serious interest from the scientific and fishing communities.

Obviously, if this behaviour continues to expand, it could become a very expensive and time-consuming problem for fishers. But it could be harmful in other ways, too. Whales, while crafty, often become caught on the hooks themselves or tied up in the lines. This causes higher mortality rates in species that don't reproduce quickly and may impact their long-term viability. Also, fish that are eaten off the line are not reported as "catch" because they are never brought onboard. When fishers then catch another full quota to replace the eaten one, this can mean that up to 50 percent of halibut or sablefish, which are tightly controlled, are not reported. This could throw off the science of fish management quite significantly.

Strategies for combatting this behaviour in predator fish are being tried, or course. Sonic deterrents, for example, seemed to work for a short period, but eventually the whales figured out the sound was harmless, and was in fact actually helpful in leading them to the more promising boats. The deterrents ended up acting as a "dinner bell" for the whales. The most effective solution so far seems to be switching the fishing method from longline to "pot" or cage-type fishing. This reduces the ability of the whales to access the fish, and almost totally eliminates whale mortality. It also tends to be a better way to fish from a conservation standpoint. It is, however, an expensive changeover, costing each boat hundreds of thousands of dollars. For now, there doesn't seem to be a better option. Mother Nature wins again.

King & Spanish Mackerel

ORIGIN: *World*

AVAILABILITY: *Year-round*

COMMON FORMS: *Fillets; steaks occasionally*

STOCK STATUS: *Good, little concern*

SOURCE: *All catch is wild*

ALTERNATIVES: *cobia, mahi-mahi, albacore tuna*

WHILE ATLANTIC MACKEREL is the most common fish of its family, and is often considered the only true mackerel, king and Spanish mackerel deserve a little attention. Spanish mackerel are perhaps more properly placed into the medium-size fish category — and can sometimes be substituted for Atlantic mackerel — but king mackerel are commonly caught at 9+ kg (20+ lb) and can grow to over 36 kg (80 lb). They are restricted to warmer waters, and are caught from North Carolina down to the Gulf of Mexico and the Caribbean. The population is healthy, and kings are recommended by all the notable oversight organizations.

Sport and recreational fishers tend to look for 13+ kg (30+ lb) fish, also known as "smokers" — so called because they are great smoked, due to their higher oil content, and will "smoke" your reel when they try to escape, as they are a fast fish. Most commercially caught fish are in the 7 to 11 kg (15 to 25 lb) range. No matter what size of king is in the fish case, you are unlikely to be buying the whole fish, so clues such as eye shine or gill colour won't be possible to ascertain. Mackerel gets soft very quickly, and will take on a notable fishy odour, as well. The flesh should be pinkish-grey and firm, and not starting to separate. As with all higher-oil fish, try to use your king as soon as possible. They do freeze pretty well, if necessary. Grilling with the skin on or pan-searing at very high heat (preferably outdoors, as it will generate a lot of smoke) are my favourite preparations for this full-flavoured fish.

LING COD

ORIGIN: *North American Pacific*

AVAILABILITY: *Year-round*

COMMON FORMS: *Fillets*

STOCK STATUS: *Some concern, but more recent conservation measures are having a positive impact*

SOURCE: *All catch is wild*

ALTERNATIVES: *cod, black cod, swordfish*

ANOTHER UGLY BUT tasty fish, ling cod are found only on the West Coast of North America and mostly around British Columbia. The ling has had its ups and downs as far as population goes, but it seems we are finally getting a handle on management. There are still some problems with certain harvest methods producing too much bycatch (for example, trawling), but steps are being taken to mitigate that, and other methods are being employed. Overall, ling cod is a delicious fish that should be enjoyed more.

Ling is a fairly long-living fish, and somewhat resembles a large eel, though you would rarely see it sold whole. Every once in a while, the flesh takes on a bright blue/green colour, depending on what that particular fish has been eating. Typically, ling caught in shallow water will be more likely to have this Smurf-like quality. Fear not, though, it's just a little extra chlorophyll, and when cooked the flesh turns a bright, snowy white and looks just as you would expect. Some say that the blue flesh is a bit sweeter, but I can't vouch for this. It's certainly not a reason to steer away from ling, though.

Grilled Ling Cod with Lime and Tarragon

Ling has a density that allows it to stand up to grilling pretty well.
Make sure the fish is well oiled, and the grill is clean and seasoned to reduce sticking.
Brush the glaze on after the fish has mostly cooked to keep it
from caramelizing or burning.

50 mL (3 tbsp + 1 tsp) high-quality
   olive oil, for glaze

Zest and juice of 2 limes

1½ tbsp (22 mL) granulated sugar

1 small bunch tarragon, leaves picked

4 pieces skin-on ling cod
   (175 g/6 oz each)

Grapeseed or other high-heat oil,
   for grilling

Kosher or rock salt, to taste

Freshly cracked black pepper, to taste

Fine or finishing salt (light flakes, not
   iodized), to taste

Get your charcoal quite hot, about 250°C (480°F), leaving a section without coals, or preheat your barbecue to high.

In a small saucepan, combine olive oil, lime zest and juice, sugar, and tarragon. Bring just to a boil, then remove from heat but keep warm, reserving a bowlful for serving alongside your grilled fish.

Brush fillets with a generous amount of grapeseed oil, and dust both sides with salt and pepper. Grill fish, skin-side down, for 5 to 6 minutes. Carefully flip over, and move to a cooler part of the grill, where the temperature is about 150°C (300°F). Grill for 3 minutes, then brush on some of the prepared glaze. Take care not to let too much hit the coals or you might have flare-ups. Cook for another 3 minutes, until the flesh flakes easily with a fork and is opaque with slight browning around the darker grill marks on the flesh side (you want the ling cod to be cooked throughout). Transfer grilled fish to serving plates and spoon remaining lime mixture onto the fillets.

Serves 4 as a light main course

─MAHI-MAHI─

ORIGIN: *Worldwide, tropical and sub-tropical waters*

AVAILABILITY: *Year-round*

COMMON FORMS: *Fillets*

STOCK STATUS: *Good, little concern, from United States only*

SOURCE: *All catch is wild*

ALTERNATIVES: *cobia, kingfish, albacore tuna*

WHEN YOU'RE NAMED "dolphin fish," there is little chance of breaking into the market. "Mahi-mahi," on the other hand, has a happier ring to it. Fished in North and South America, mahi-mahi is also an extremely popular sport fish. In fact, much weight is given to the recreational fishery when establishing annual catch limits. It's technically available year-round, but American mahi-mahi sometimes has limited availability from late summer to January. Be very careful when purchasing during this period, as the Peruvian and Ecuadorian mahi fisheries are still under review, and management is a lot less stringent there than in the States. Always purchase American mahi-mahi.

When it comes to many of the larger, firm-fleshed fish, such as mahi and swordfish, it's very important to remove the bloodline — the dark band of flesh that runs along the length of the fish, which has a slightly stronger flavour. To remove the bloodline, use a sharp pointy knife to cut down about 1 cm (½ inch) away from the red tint in the flesh into the whole width of the bloodline. It is quite apparent which parts of the flesh are permeated by the bloodline, as they will be quite dark red. Do this on both sides of the bloodline,

then cut around the bottom if it does not penetrate the whole fillet. Sometimes you will have to cut the piece into two portions to remove larger bloodlines.

Typically when buying mahi, I'll ask for a chunk of fish so I can portion it out myself. If the fish shop portions the fish for me, it can be tough to remove the bits of bloodline without massacring the fillets. It's also best to remove the skin prior to cooking. The flesh should look pinkish-white, and the fillets should be tight without any gaping between grains. If you can see the bloodline, and it has gone dark brown, it may be a clue that the fish is not as fresh as it could be. Give it a good smell before buying.

The flavour of mahi is similar to albacore tuna or kingfish. It's great grilled or cooked in the pan with stronger spices. I've served it raw, but you should know that mahi is not as mild in flavour as some other fish.

—SALMON—

ORIGIN: *Worldwide, mostly northern hemisphere*

AVAILABILITY: *Year-round*

COMMON FORMS: *Whole; fillets*

STOCK STATUS: *Wild fisheries are pretty tightly controlled and should be trusted; farmed product*

SOURCE: *Healthy amount of catch is wild, though majority available is farmed*

ALTERNATIVES: *trout, char*

THE TOPIC OF salmon certainly merits its own book. Easily the most important fish in North America, and one of the top fish worldwide, salmon's historical importance can't be overstated. The emotions salmon elicits are powerful, especially from the "wild only" groups. When speaking about cultivated salmon, we are mostly referring to a select few varieties: Atlantic (even when grown in the Pacific), chinook (or spring), and coho. Norway, Chile, Scotland, and Canada account for a little over 90 percent of all farmed salmon, with the United States, Australia, Faroe Islands, and Ireland responsible for most of the rest. About 70 percent of the world's salmon supply (all varieties) comes from aquaculture, with 30 percent coming from the various wild species.

Wild varieties of salmon include pink, coho, sockeye (red and Copper River), chinook (spring, king, and ivory), and chum (keta). Wild harvesting occurs mainly in Russia, Canada, the United States, and Japan. Together, these four countries account for well over 90 percent of the total wild production worldwide. Unlike farmed salmon, which is available year-round, one of the main drawbacks of choosing wild product is that it is seasonal. Unfortunately, some farmed fish has been mislabelled as wild due to a general lack of awareness about salmon seasons. In general, if a fish is listed on a menu as simply "salmon," it is likely farmed fish.

Due to its rapid expansion and recent large-scale introduction, farmed salmon tends to have a poor reputation. Of course, some people will never eat a farmed fish; but, for the rest of us, it's important to understand that, as with any industry, there are good practices and poor ones.

If we want to continue eating salmon, we are going to have to make peace with the fact that some of the fish we eat will be farmed.

If we want to continue eating salmon, we are going to have to make peace with the fact that some of the fish we eat will be farmed. I don't look at this as a negative, just a matter of education.

One of the main arguments against raising piscivorous (fish-eating) fish in a farm setting is that we are taking otherwise usable fish out of the global supply to inefficiently feed more desirable fish. This is true to a certain extent, but the fact remains that most of us are not going to start eating menhaden or anchovies, so we are converting this otherwise inessential and unwelcome fish into one that we are going to eat. Fish meal production has remained stable over the past few years. It used to go into livestock feed, but more and more it is just being diverted to feeding fish instead.

Fish escapes and pollution from cages have been issues, as well, but as with any young industry, these problems are being solved — sometimes more slowly than we'd like, of course. Land-based recirculation systems, allowing cage sites to go fallow, and other strategies are helping to mitigate some of the most serious concerns. Overall, good farmed salmon is available, and it's just as healthy as wild. Keep in mind that it will be more expensive than we have been accustomed to paying. It's best to stop looking for the best deal on salmon, and start looking for the best salmon, period — be it wild or farmed.

It can be tricky to remember all the particulars of fishing seasons, but be aware that no wild salmon is caught in December, and the supply of all fresh wild salmon is very small, with the exception of chinook, throughout the winter months. If you see wild sockeye for sale in February, for example, it will either be frozen (not a bad thing, just not "fresh," and shouldn't be sold as such) or mislabelled.

Sean Dimin of Sea to Table shows off a large Amberjack in Beaufort, N.C.

A New Way to Get Fish to Your Table

Sea to Table started in Brooklyn in the mid-2000s with a goal of making delicious, sustainably caught seafood available to everyone. Since then, they have pioneered a new model of breaking down the barriers between restaurants, consumers, and fishers. Recently, I sat down with the president of Sea to Table, Sean Dimin.

JOHN: Can a fishery be too remote? Do you have a limit where it no longer makes sense for you to work with it?

SEAN: We only work with U.S. domestic fisheries. In order to ship fresh fish overnight to chefs, we depend on our trusted partners — the people who work the boats and the docks. It's not always just that a certain fish is 16 or 22 hours out of the water. It's about the handling of the fish, and the respect and care that goes into it. There's a standard that starts right at the dock. Of course, selling fresh fish has its costs and its limitations, so we also sell a lot of our fish frozen. It's how we overcome seasonality, and it's how we drive down the costs of distribution. And it's how I eat fish. I don't ship myself fresh fish from all over the country to have dinner each night. It's just not a reasonable way to live. But I do want to eat fish all the time. So properly frozen fish is the answer.

We work with some seriously remote places, but with the right freezing technology, you could be fishing off the farthest key in Florida or Nome, Alaska, and as long you don't have a rush on the fish, so that it gets frozen properly, you can still get it to market and be able to tell that story of where it came from and have super-high quality.

A real pleasure of my job is travelling to different communities and meeting with the fishers. I love it. When I started the business, I went out on the boats more often, and I still beg to, but they always drag me back to the office. Most fishing communities are remote. They're not near major metropolitan areas. They've been pushed out to remote areas of our country, and they're being overtaken by marinas and condos. Waterfront property is getting so expensive, how could you run a fish plant or dock fishing boats?

JOHN: Do you work with lionfish?

SEAN: That's a fun one. There's a clear environmental problem with an invasive species that can really only be combatted through harvest. So what do you do with it? You don't want to waste it; you want to monetize it. But they're expensive. It costs hundreds of dollars to go out on a boat with scuba tanks, and go out diving and spearing them one at a time. But it gets people involved, and it gets people knowledgeable about issues around the ocean and fishing. So something like lionfish, to us, is pure fun. And we do quite a bit of it through the Gulf, Florida, and Southeast Atlantic. Really, we get as much as we can.

JOHN: I push mackerel a lot. For so many years, it was a bait fish and it was treated pretty poorly on the boats. It was just brought in and left there; nobody even iced it down, because it was just going in the lobster traps a couple of days later. But more and more, I've been finding pretty good mackerel, and I'm wondering if fishers are starting to understand that there's more value in certain fish if they treat them a bit better?

SEAN: Definitely. It's hard with mackerel because the biomass is so large and dominated by big trawlers. But the stuff coming out of Chatham and Cape Cod is all hook and line.

JOHN: Would you consider supplying a Costco-style operation, or is that something you don't even mix with?

SEAN: We currently don't sell into any retail. We're concerned with keeping good controls over both our supplies and where our products go. But the mission of the business is to get every American to eat healthy, delicious, affordable, and sustainable fish. So, whatever the outlet, as long as it's supporting that goal and the quality that we are proud of, that's where we want to go with this. We want to be a large-scale, impactful solution.

JOHN: Did you come from a fishing background?

SEAN: Not professionally. I grew up fishing with my grandfather on the South Shore, near Long Island. I spent some time up on Cape Cod with my mom's family. I grew up in a town full of lakes. I fished as much as you possibly could, but I can't really call myself a fisher. I think it was just a confluence of passion, between fishing and the water, the people around it, and food. One of our advantages is that we didn't come from seafood, so we think about it differently. We don't think about volume; we think about value. We don't think about commoditized products; we think about storytelling.

JOHN: Can chefs or restaurants have an impact on changing what people want?

SEAN: I think chefs are an integral part of this. There's so much interest in food and the culinary world across different media. We just have to open people's eyes to a few key concepts: Buy fish that comes from somewhere, that comes from someone. Ask the questions. Fish tastes better if it has a story or comes from a good place. That's the message I push. The best advice you can give someone trying to source sustainably is to ask the uncomfortable questions, whether you're at the supermarket, the fish counter, or a restaurant. If you see an unfamiliar fish on the menu, ask where it came from. And if they don't have the answer, they're going to get flustered, they're going to go ask someone else. The server is going to go ask the chef, and if the chef doesn't know the answer, they're going to get embarrassed and ask their supplier. And if the supplier doesn't have the answer, hopefully the chef fires the supplier and finds someone he can trust. And that little chain reaction, that butterfly effect, will really drive things forward.

JOHN: Do you think the existing safeguards can be weakened, or do you think they're strong enough that they can survive eight years of the wrong oversight?

SEAN: It's a scary thought, but my hope is that between science, management, and producers, enough trust has been built up over the last 15 or 20 years that any deregulation coming from the federal level will be ignored. We know we're in this together, and we've been down that road before. We want to make sure the fisheries are still here tomorrow, that they're here for our kids.

JOHN: You deal with a lot of fishers. In your mind, is the life getting too hard? Is there still money there for people, enough to make a living?

SEAN: The market's really lagging behind. But I think that when people realize the true value of seafood, they will support the fisheries even more, and it will get better. But it's hard times. There's money to be made, but it's for the people who are truly dedicated. It's not something you can skip off to and get rich quick. Nobody's getting rich in seafood.

JOHN: Do you deal with aquaculture at all? And if not, is there a reason why?

SEAN: Just shellfish, oysters really. Our clams are wild, our mussels are wild. But shellfish isn't huge for us. We're more finfish. It's expensive shipping shellfish across the country. You're basically shipping rocks.

Right now, our message really is: U.S., wild-caught, sustainable, traceable. I think aquaculture is a necessity, and an inevitable solution to feeding the world's people, but there are far too few really good examples of aquaculture being done right, especially on the finfish side. There is a lot of learning and growth needed there.

JOHN: Would Sea to Table be able to grow enough to provide a solution for everybody?

SEAN: It makes us happiest when people start asking for the right things. And if we can be a part of it, that's great. We are not the solution to the world's seafood problems, but hopefully we can be part of a solution. Hopefully, we can be a guiding light to get people to ask for the right stuff. The problem — and the solution — is so much bigger than any one player. And we are only talking about U.S. markets and U.S. supply, just one part of the overall world.

STRIPED BASS

ORIGIN: *North America, mostly Atlantic, some freshwater, and Pacific*

AVAILABILITY: *Farmed, year-round; wild, typically May to September*

COMMON FORMS: *Whole; fillets*

STOCK STATUS: *Good, strictly managed; farming is a growing source of fish*

SOURCE: *Much of the catch is wild, though aquaculture is increasing*

ALTERNATIVES: *pickerel, bream, sea bass*

FEW FISH EXCITE fishers and chefs in the Northeast like the striped bass. In fact, so esteemed is it as a sport fish, that it is one of the few commercially desirable fish actually caught in significantly greater numbers recreationally than commercially. Between 75 to 80 percent of (saltwater) striped bass, about 26 million pounds, landed in the United States goes to sport fishers, with the remaining 6 million pounds sold commercially. Some aquaculture production of freshwater striped bass exists, and this effort is growing, but the wild fishery still accounts for almost half of the fish sold in restaurants and shops.

Striped bass ranges from southern Nova Scotia down to the Gulf of Mexico, and from California to British Columbia. There are also freshwater populations in many states. Most of the commercially available wild fish come from Chesapeake Bay up to Massachusetts. Currently, there is no significant commercial fishery in Canada. Striped bass is usually available from mid-May until the various quotas are filled, typically in September. There is no fishing allowed in federally controlled waters (between 3 miles and 200 miles from shore), so each state controls its own fishing season. The wild striped bass fishery on the East Coast is considered well managed by almost everyone, and though this fish tends to be a little pricy, it's definitely worth it.

— SAFFRON-POACHED STRIPED BASS —

The beauty of getting a whole striped bass is that they are usually big enough to share and once you lift the fillets from the fish, the bones make an amazing broth to poach the fish in.

1 striped bass (1.8 to 2.25 kg/4 to 5 lb), whole or filleted, bone-in (allow about 500g/1 lb fish per person)

4 to 5 L (16 to 20 cups) water

3 stalks celery, cut widthwise into 3 pieces

1 onion, quartered

1 carrot, halved lengthwise

4 bay leaves

60 mL (¼ cup) salt

20 whole black peppercorns

10 g (0.35 oz) saffron threads

Debone the fish, reserving the bones and fillets separately. Cut fillets into 4 even portions and rinse well under cold running water. Set aside. (Although it's improbable that the fish will spoil when left at room temperature for less than an hour, it would be safest to put it back in the fridge.)

In a large pot, combine water, celery, onion, carrot, bay leaves, salt, and peppercorns. Add reserved fish bones. Bring water to a rolling boil, then reduce heat to low and simmer for 45 minutes.

Using a fine-mesh sieve, strain stock into a clean pot. Discard solids. (It's important to strain your fish stock well. After you remove it from the heat, you can let it settle for 30 minutes or so, to help.)

Cook strained stock over high heat until it's reduced to about 1 L (4 cups). Remove from heat and add saffron. Let steep for 15 minutes.

Place pot over medium-low heat and bring to a low simmer. Gently add reserved fillets. Poach fillets for 6 to 8 minutes, until flesh is opaque. Remove pot from heat. Quickly divide fish among four wide serving bowls, or six to eight smaller bowls. Pour poaching liquid over each. Serve immediately.

Serves 4 as a main or 6 to 8 as an appetizer

STURGEON

ORIGIN: *Worldwide*

AVAILABILITY: *Year-round*

COMMON FORMS: *Whole; fillets*

STOCK STATUS: *Highly variable depending on jurisdiction: wild is mostly to be avoided, except from well-managed North American sources; farmed fish are typically okay from the United States, Canada, and Italy*

SOURCE: *Most of the catch is farmed; small amounts of wild fish tightly controlled*

ALTERNATIVES: *ivory salmon, mahi-mahi*

ONE OF THE most legendary and problematic fisheries in the world, sturgeon is the most sought after — and to some, the only "true" — source of caviar. But its meat is also wonderful, particularly smoked, when it acquires an almost ham-like quality. There are a few wild populations of sturgeon that are still considered suitable for harvest, namely white sturgeon from the West Coast of the United States, and lake sturgeon from the St. Lawrence and Saint John river systems. But the volume of fish taken from these areas is small, and not nearly sufficient to supply worldwide demand.

The main problem with assessing wild sturgeon stocks and their stability is that the fish live remarkably long lives — many varieties live more than 100 years — but do not begin to reproduce until they are well into their teens. The more we can do to protect these gorgeous fish, the better. Happily, because of their value and lifestyle, sturgeon lend themselves to successful cultivation, both in lakes and recirculation systems. China, the United Arab Emirates, and Italy currently combine to produce over 70 tons of farmed caviar annually, representing more than 60 percent of the world's supply, with countries such as the United States, Uruguay, and Canada contributing smaller amounts. All of these producers also supply sturgeon meat, as this is now

considered a valuable part of the fish, as opposed to the more cavalier treatment the meat received when eggs were being wild harvested on the Caspian Sea. This is a positive outcome of the evolution of the sturgeon industry, as we are now more likely to see sturgeon in fish shops, in addition to the caviar, and all of it can be eaten guilt-free. As always, though, I recommend focusing on sturgeon (and eggs) from trustworthy countries, such as the United States, Canada, and Italy.

Sturgeon meat is very easy to handle, and is perfect for grilling, smoking, and chowder, as it holds together well when cooked and has a relatively high oil content, ensuring that it won't dry out as quickly as more delicate fish. It's fine to cook fillets with the skin on, but it should be removed prior to serving, as it is inedible.

— Smoked Sturgeon Chowder —

*Smoke much more sturgeon than you need for this, and freeze it.
It will keep well for 6 months, possibly longer. If you are feeling particularly fancy,
try garnishing the soup with some caviar. It won't necessarily add anything to the chowder,
but it will add to your guests' happiness. Try it, if you don't believe me.*

For smoking the fish:

4 L (16 cups) cold water

250 mL (1 cup) kosher salt

250 mL (1 cup) pure maple syrup
  or brown sugar

1 medium onion, chopped

20 whole black peppercorns

4 bay leaves

1 sturgeon fillet (400 g to 3 kg/14 oz
  to 6.6 lb)

For the chowder:

30 mL (2 tbsp) vegetable oil

4 medium shallots, minced

2 stalks celery, tops removed,
  finely minced

2 medium potatoes, peeled and cut
  into small cubes

1 L (4 cups) fish stock or clam stock

3 sprigs fresh thyme, picked

400 g (14 oz) smoked sturgeon, cut
  into small cubes

2 L (8 cups) heavy or whipping
  (35%) cream

To smoke the fish: First, make a brine: In a large bowl, combine water, salt, maple syrup or brown sugar, onion, peppercorns, and bay leaves. Stir until salt is completely dissolved. Gently place fillet into brine, cover, and refrigerate for 1 to 2 hours.

Remove fish from brine, place on a platter, and let dry, uncovered, in the fridge for at least 1 hour and up to 24 hours.

Place sturgeon in a smoker that is running between 40 and 80°C (104 to 176°F). Smoke for 90 minutes if smoker is at 80°C, and up to 4 hours if smoker is at 40°C (104°F). The fish should take on a slight golden hue but not dry out too much.

To make the chowder: In a medium stockpot, over medium-low heat, heat oil. Add shallots and celery, and cook, stirring occasionally, for 15 minutes, until vegetables are softened but not browned. Add potatoes and fish stock, and reduce heat to low. Cook, stirring occasionally, until potatoes are tender but not mushy. Stir in thyme, smoked sturgeon, and cream, and warm mixture to desired temperature, very gently. Do not let soup boil over.

Serves 4 to 6

—SWORDFISH—

ORIGIN: *Worldwide*

AVAILABILITY: *Year-round*

COMMON FORMS: *Fillets*

STOCK STATUS: *North American fisheries are
well managed overall; not recommended outside of North America*

SOURCE: *All catch is wild*

ALTERNATIVES: *halibut, mahi-mahi*

IN RECENT YEARS, the desire for swordfish has dropped significantly. The fishery is healthier than it's been in a long time, with extremely selective and sustainable methods of harvesting (such as harpooning) making a strong comeback. Pricing is lower than for halibut, which is a very comparable fish, both in taste and aesthetics. So, what gives?

Back in the late '90s, a campaign called "Give Swordfish a Break" brought to light many issues facing the fishery. It was deemed successful and stopped in 2000. However, fisheries outside of North America are still problematic, so this might have a lingering impact on perception and sales. But the main reason for the recent unpopularity of swordfish, it would seem, is the level of mercury potentially contained in its flesh. This is obviously a very emotional issue for a lot of people, and is subject to conflicting advice, even from government sources. The average levels of mercury found in swordfish are still under one part per million. Although it is not recommended for children and pregnant women, it is otherwise within safe limits for everyone else. Of course, many organizations feel that the overall benefits of eating fish outweigh the potential problems. It's also true that no one will make their entire fish diet consist of higher-mercury fish, such as swordfish and tilefish. Occasional consumption shouldn't pose a problem for most people, though of course the choice is very personal.

— Poached Swordfish in Olive Oil —

The hardest aspect of cooking swordfish is controlling moisture.
It's a great fish, and I love its flavour, but it can dry out very quickly if you're
not careful. This is my foolproof method for avoiding that fate.

4 portions skinless swordfish (each 175 g/6 oz and 2.5 cm/1 inch thick, or even a bit thicker)

Salt and pepper, to taste

1 L (4 cups) good but not great olive oil

2 to 3 sprigs fresh thyme

4 cloves garlic

Peel of 1 lemon

Leave fish on the counter for about an hour to bring it to room temperature, then season all over with salt and pepper.

Preheat oven to about 80°C (170°F). Find a pot that will comfortably fit the fish, without stacking or having the pieces touch.

In pot, over medium-high heat, combine oil, thyme, garlic, and lemon peel. Heat until oil reaches 50°C (122°F). Add fish, being careful to keep at least a tiny bit of space between pieces. Transfer pot to preheated oven. Cook for 20 minutes, and then check for doneness. One method I use to check for doneness without cutting into a portion is to put an extra cube of fish, about 3 cm (1¼ inches) square in the oil so I can just pull it out and cut it open to see if I'm happy. If you aren't yet happy with the texture, you can cook it for an additional 5 minutes or so. Cook for no longer than 30 minutes total, though.

Once fish is cooked to your liking, remove fish from oil and briefly let drain on a kitchen towel or a couple of layers of paper towel. Serve with your favourite veggies.

Serves 4 as a light main course

TO GRILL OR NOT TO GRILL?

I'm a big fan of harpooned swordfish myself, and will cook it as simply as possible. I find that it does have a tendency to dry out if cooked too long or at high heat. To me, the ideal cooking method is to sear the pieces of fish in a very hot pan for perhaps just 2 minutes per side, and then to finish the fish in a moderate oven (around 150°C/300°F) for an additional 5 or 6 minutes. This preparation yields a much juicier result and is more tolerant of errors in timing. If you throw the swordfish directly on the grill, a lot of the natural juices will drip right off, and you will be left with dry fish.

—TILEFISH—

ORIGIN: *Worldwide*
AVAILABILITY: *Year-round*
COMMON FORMS: *Fillets*
STOCK STATUS: *Good, little concern,*
except for grey or blueline; look for golden tilefish
SOURCE: *All catch is wild*
ALTERNATIVES: *grouper, monkfish*

TILEFISH IS A beautiful fish, with an undeserved reputation for being fragile and difficult to handle. Similar in character to grouper, the flesh of the golden tilefish is meaty with large flakes and a moderate amount of fat. It loves poaching and rich sauces. Recent studies have shown there is absolutely no danger in Atlantic-caught tilefish, and quite possibly in fish sourced in the Gulf of Mexico. As an added bonus, most of the fishery is well managed, with tight controls and responsible practices. A tiny bit of confusion occurs between the two main varieties of tilefish and how they are named: Golden tilefish are also known as "blue tilefish," and have a healthy population. Grey tilefish are otherwise known as "blueline tilefish," and these are highly restricted with a recommendation not to purchase. It would be easier if people had been a little more creative naming these two varieties back in the day, but unfortunately we're stuck with these names.

Tilefish tend to be fairly large fish, often 9+ kg (20+ lb), so you will most likely find them already portioned. The flesh is pinkish-white and may contain some pin bones that need to be removed, though these tend to be easy to spot. It's better, if possible, to get fillets from a larger fish, even if they might be a bit pricier. Larger fish tend to have a longer shelf life and are a bit firmer. In general, look for firm fillets with a tight grain and a clean smell. Cooking with the skin on is highly recommended, and the skin is perfectly edible, though I usually remove the scales.

TILEFISH WITH ROAST TOMATOES AND GRITS

Shrimp and grits is a popular dish down South, but I see no reason not to pair the firm and juicy tilefish with this sweet side dish and some oven-roasted tomatoes.

For the roast tomatoes:

6 to 8 Roma or San Marzano tomatoes, cut into rounds

60 mL (¼ cup) olive oil

1 bunch fresh oregano, leaves only

Salt and pepper, to taste

For the grits:

400 mL (1⅔ cups) water, divided

125 mL (½ cup) whole milk

125 mL (½ cup) hominy grits

15 mL (1 tbsp) salt

50 mL (3 tbsp + 1 tsp) butter

For the fish:

4 portions tilefish (150 to 175g/5 to 6 oz each), skin-on, if possible

100 mL (6 tbsp + 2 tsp) grapeseed or other high-heat oil

Salt and pepper, to taste

To roast the tomatoes: Preheat oven to 190°C (375°F). Line a baking sheet with parchment paper.

In a bowl, combine sliced tomatoes and a generous amount of olive oil. Sprinkle with oregano, salt, and pepper. Arrange in an even layer on prepared baking sheet and roast in preheated oven for about 40 minutes.

To make the grits: While tomatoes are roasting, in a medium saucepan over medium-high heat, combine 375 mL (1½ cups) of the water and all of the milk. Bring to a very slow boil so as not to curdle the milk. Add grits, and cook, whisking, for just under a minute, scraping the sides and bottom of the pan as needed. Reduce heat to low, cover, and cook for an additional 20 minutes, adding remaining water, salt, and butter, about halfway through. Remove from heat.

To make the fish: In a sauté pan, heat oil over medium-high heat. When oil shines, sprinkle salt on the skin side of the fish, and then lay the fish, skin-side down, in the pan. Sear for about 5 minutes. Remove pan from heat, and season top of fillet with salt and pepper.

Place fillets, skin-side up, on top of roast tomatoes, still on sheet pan. Return pan to oven, and cook for 5 to 6 minutes, until the skin is slightly brown and the flesh is firm and opaque.

Remove pan from oven. Divide grits evenly between four plates and arrange fillets on top. Using a spoon, stir together the tomatoes and juices on the pan, and spoon mixture over each serving of fish. Serve immediately.

Serves 4 as a main course

Storing Seafood

MOLLUSKS

Generally speaking, mollusks are characterized by having a protective shell of some form, although some groups have evolved to the point where their shell is now a beak, such as squid and octopuses, or internalized, such as slugs.

When handling and storing fresh squid and octopus, it's important not to let them sit in any of the liquid that will inevitably collect around them for more than a day. Once cleaned, the flesh should be patted dry and then stored in a clean container lined with a dry kitchen towel. Cover the container with a lid and refrigerate until you are ready to prepare it. Stored this way, squid and octopus will keep well for up to 3 days.

There are two broad groups of mollusks, each of which sports an external shell: univalves, which have a single-section shell (such as periwinkles and snails) and bivalves, which have two hinged sections to their shell (such as scallops, mussels, and clams).

The most important factor in determining the safe handling and storage of mollusks is how hard, or thick, the shell is: Thicker and harder shelled mollusks are more likely to have a longer "shelf life" (the length of time the animal will live outside of its natural environment). Most species of shellfish thrive in intertidal areas and subsequently have evolved to live out of water for a certain amount of time — this is also key to their shelf life. As all commercially sold shellfish must be accompanied by some record of when they were harvested and packed for shipping, you should be able to get this information at point of purchase, which will help you determine whether the seafood you are buying is indeed fresh. Most mollusks usually go on a 2- to 3-day journey, from packing to market. During shipping, they must be kept cold, safe from extreme temperatures, in refrigerated trailers or insulated coolers with icepacks.

Softer shelled mollusks, such as mussels, geoduck, and soft-shell and razor clams, have a shelf life of at least 3 to 4 days from point of purchase — this adds up to about a week out of the water. Thinner shelled animals are much more likely to open and close out of water, which allows the life-sustaining liquids in their shells to leak out, eventually causing the animal to die. In fact, a gaped or opened shell can be an indicator that a mollusk has died, although it is important to note that all mollusks can gape and still be alive. A living mollusk will close shut when given a hard tap on the shell. If it does not close, then it's either dead or dying and must be discarded. Similarly, live soft-shelled clams may have a siphon protruding from their shells. If you gently touch this part with a finger, the clam will suck the member back in. If it does not, the animal is dead or dying and should be discarded.

When you get home with your purchased mussels and soft-shelled clams, it's best to take them out of the container they came in. If you are not going to cook them immediately, check for and discard any broken or dead ones, give the remainder a rinse under cold running water, and then put them into a clean container, cover with a cold, damp towel, and refrigerate right away.

Soft-shelled mollusks will often spew out liquid during shipping and storage, and this liquid will spoil rather quickly, even under refrigerated conditions. For this reason, if you plan to store soft-shelled mollusks for more than a day or so, it is advisable to check daily for any accumulation of this usually brown liquid in the container and, if present, rinse the shellfish and transfer them to a clean container. In commercial settings where larger volumes of these shellfish are stored, they use a double container system to keep things fresh: A container with a perforated bottom holds the shellfish, allowing the liquid to drain into a solid container underneath it.

Live scallops are sometimes available, and like thin-shelled mussels and clams, they tend to open rather easily when exposed to the air. Store them as described above, but don't expect them to last for more than a couple of days after purchase. Shucked scallops, which is how they are sold most often, should be stored in the same way as squid and octopus. When freshly shucked, scallop meat has a clear, almost translucent white tone, with a hint of pink or orange. Within a couple of days, shucked scallops will start to exude a somewhat ammonia-scented liquid and turn opaque. This is normal, but if they sit in this liquid for more than a day or two, they will become quite sour to the taste. To reduce the accumulation of this liquid, pat them dry and store them wrapped in a clean kitchen towel. Unfortunately, in most markets, scallops sold as "fresh" were shipped frozen, then thawed before being presented for sale. It's usually best to purchase frozen scallop meat and then thaw it out in the fridge over a day or two.

For thinly shelled univalve or single-shelled mollusks such as snails and periwinkles, it's very difficult to discern if they are alive in the shell. If any limp and unmoving part of the body is sticking out, the animal is dead and most likely spoiled or spoiling, and should be discarded. Unless they are giving off a somewhat putrid smell when you get home, there is no need to rinse them. Simply transfer them to a clean container, place a damp towel on them, and refrigerate. They will be fine in the fridge for a couple of days.

For mollusks with thicker and harder shells, such as oysters, quahogs, and other hard-shell clams, handling and storage is a little simpler, and they keep longer than their more fragile cousins. These animals are intertidal creatures equipped to live exposed to the air for certain periods of time. Their ability to sustain themselves out of the water is somewhat reduced in warmer summer months, but as a rule larger hard-shell clams will thrive for a couple of weeks after harvesting, as will most oysters (often for up to a month). The older and subsequently bigger animals have larger and stronger adductor muscles and can remain firmly closed for longer periods of time.

Once these shellfish are purchased and brought home, there is no need to rinse them unless a somewhat putrid smell dictates. Discard any that are gaping open if they do not close upon being tapped, then simply place them in a container, cover with a damp kitchen towel, and store in the coldest part of your fridge. If you plan on storing oysters for more than a couple of days, it's best to arrange them with the more rounded part of the shell, called the cup, face down in the container. This will help the liquid inside remain settled within the shell and prevent it from dripping out if the animal gapes open.

CRUSTACEANS

The handling and storage of crustaceans, which includes lobsters, crabs, and shrimp, varies markedly. Lobsters and crabs are usually purchased alive and will stay alive for a couple of days in the fridge. Keeping them in a plastic or cardboard container is best. If they are delivered in a styrofoam container, give them a rinse under cold water and then transfer them to a better container, as above. Cooked lobster and crab meat taken out of the shell will keep in an airtight container in the fridge for 3 days. If you are refrigerating whole, cooked lobster, store them on their backs as it helps to contain any liquid within.

If you are able to buy live shrimp or prawns, it's best to cook them same day, before they start dying, although they are still very good for up to 3 days after dying. Simply store them in an airtight container in the fridge and check them daily to make sure no acrid smell is developing. At the first hint of a strong smell, rinse the shrimp under cold running water and cook them. Cooked shrimp will keep in an airtight container in the refrigerator for up to 3 days but are best eaten the same day they are cooked. The head portions of shrimp and prawns will spoil first, so if you are not preparing them for a couple of days, it's best to cut the heads off before storing them.

FINFISH

The handling and storage of finfish is the same for most species, and only changes depending on the size of the fish and whether it is whole or filleted.

The best gauge of fish quality is smell, as the human nose is very well equipped to detect even the slightest odours of spoiling fish. Fresh, edible fish has almost no smell, and any strong sulphur or ammonia scent is a sure indication that the fish has gone bad. With all fish, the less it's handled, the better. Most contamination comes from touching and exposing the fish. If you are going to prepare the fish the day you buy it, simply leave it in the packaging it's in and refrigerate until ready to cook. Otherwise, follow the advice below.

WHOLE FISH

Whole fish require the most careful handling, as residue of blood and cuts will spoil before the flesh will. Whole fish will also often have slime forming on the skin, which spoils quickly. The best practice is to wash whole fish inside and out under cold running water as soon as possible after getting home. Once it's washed, it is very important to pat it dry and then refrigerate it. If you are not preparing it that day, put a dry kitchen towel in the bottom of a suitable container and place the clean, dry fish on top of it. Cover the container with a proper lid or plastic wrap. Blood and other liquids will continue to leach from the flesh, so if you are leaving it in the fridge for more than a day it's best to check it and change the towel if any liquid has accumulated. Do not let any form of fish, whole or otherwise, sit in a container where liquids have accumulated, as these will spoil quickly and will contaminate the skin and flesh.

FISH FILLETS

Fillets of fish require the least amount of care when storing for more than a day or two. If you are storing fillets for more than 2 days, remove them from the packaging, rinse under cold running water, pat dry, and then place in an airtight container. If the fillets are very small and delicate (like perch or sole), do not rinse them. Loosely lay a piece of plastic wrap on top of the fillets in the container to help retain moisture.

Tightly wrapping fillets in plastic — as seen in sushi bar display cases and grocery stores — is useful when the fish is somewhat exposed and handled often, but not necessary at home. Fillets that have been left for too long will begin to break apart as they dry up. The fish is still edible at this point but must be cooked immediately.

How to Clean and Fillet a Fish

The cleaning of fish and their "filleting" — the term for removing the flesh from the bones — is a practice that most people can go a lifetime without indulging in. However, if you want to experience the pleasures of eating fresh-caught or whole fish from the market, it is a skill well worth acquiring. Not only will handling the whole fish help you understand its form and freshness, but cutting it up will also expose you to all the nuances in the density and texture of the flesh — the surest way to learn how to properly prepare fish.

Needless to say, there are many forms of fish, and each type requires a somewhat different method. Despite the variations, certain broad characteristics are common to most fish, so a general approach to cleaning and filleting can be applied with success.

SCALING

If you want to remove the scales from the fish, it's best to do it first, before gutting the fish, when the body is a little more rigid and can better withstand the vigorous scaling action. Most fishmongers will do it for you if you ask, but it is handy to know how to do it yourself. You'll need a fish scaler or simply the back of a knife.

1. To scale the fish, lay it on its side, with the tail facing your dominant hand.

2. Using a kitchen towel to protect your other hand, hold the fish by the head near the gills. Starting at the tail end, using your tool of choice, scrape the scales from tail to head (against the scales) in repeated strokes. The scales should easily fly off. Flip the fish over and repeat until all of the scales have been removed (the fish should feel smooth to the touch).

3. Rinse your scaled fish under cool running water, and pat dry with paper towel or a clean kitchen towel. It's now ready to be cleaned.

CLEANING OR GUTTING

Fish are mostly muscle or flesh, and the bulk of their organs and the digestive system are gathered in the softer front section of the animal, below and behind the head and gills, and running all the way to the anal fin, which is located a bit more than halfway along the underside of the animal. To clean or gut the fish, follow these steps using a sharp, ideally thin-bladed, knife:

1. Place the fish on a cutting board with its belly facing you and locate the fish's anal fin. With the edge of the knife blade facing the head, insert the tip of the knife about ½ cm (¼ inch) into the belly, on the head side of the anal fin.

2. Working carefully, cut the belly all the way to the centre of the gills. Pull the knife out and set it aside. Most of the innards will now be exposed.

3. To remove the guts from the cavity, hold the body of the fish down with one hand. Using two fingers from your other hand, reach into the head end of the cut (which is where you will find the beginning of the digestive system) and grasp the tubes with your fingers. In a fluid motion, push your fingers up into the back of the fish and then pull your hand toward the anal fin to scoop out as much of the loose matter as you can (a bit of blood, but mostly the stomach, intestines, and organs); discard this matter unless you have some use for the heart and liver. Repeat the process until the cavity is empty. You should now be able to see and feel the bones of the fish's symmetrical skeleton (in general, a backbone and a series of ribs that run down from it).

4. Rinse the cavity under cool running water, making sure to use your fingers to scrape away any remaining bits of tissue.

5. If you plan on cooking the fish whole, it's best to cut out the gills at this point: Insert the point of the knife into the part of the gill closest to the mouth of the fish. Carefully cut into and around the gill structure until you can remove the whole gill. Repeat on the other side. You should also cut off any fins. Discard the gills and fins. Rinse the cavities under cool running water. Using a clean kitchen towel or rag, pat dry both the inside and outside of the fish.

6. To fillet the fish, you'll need to cut off the head: Resting the fish on its side, place your knife just behind the gill cavity and, using a modicum of force, cut through the backbone to sever the head from the body. On some larger fish, such as cod, it's worth spending the time to cut out the fleshy parts of the head, like the cheeks.

FILLETING

After scaling and cleaning the fish, you should now be left with the empty body of the fish lying on its side. Having looked into the cavity of the fish when cleaning it, you will have some sense of how the backbone and the hanging ribs support the fleshy part of the tapering body: The flesh is thickest where the head has been severed and slims down to the tail.

1. Place your non-dominate hand flat on the fish to keep it steady. Using your other hand, position the centre part of your knife blade (a sharp, narrow blade works best) lengthwise just slightly above the backbone and ribs of the fish. In long, sweeping motions, carefully cut the flesh from head to tail, letting the blade slip out the narrow end just before the tail. Ideally, the flesh should come off in one piece (this is your first fillet); set it aside. Flip the fish over and repeat.

2. Once the two fillets have been removed, only the skeleton with bits of flesh between the bones should remain. Save this, along with the gill-less head, for making stock, if you wish.

3. Many varieties of fish, especially those in the salmon and trout families, have a series of very fine bones — called pin bones — that run through the meat about one-third of the way up from the stomach. You can sometimes see them or more easily feel them by running your fingertips gently along the bottom half of the fillet. These bones must be removed: You can either pull them out with your fingertips or a pair of tweezers.

REMOVING THE SKIN

Many types of fish can be cooked and eaten with the skin on, but if you'd like to remove the skin from your fillets, here's how:

1. Place the fillet skin-side down on a cutting board. Using your non-dominant hand, hold the narrow (tail) end of the fillet between two fingers (use a kitchen towel to prevent slipping). Holding the knife at a 45-degree angle about 1 cm (½ inch) from the tail end, cut into the fillet just to — but not through — the skin.

2. Turn the blade of the knife until it is as parallel to the board as possible. Keeping a firm grasp on the tail end, carefully cut the flesh away from the skin using a slight up-and-down motion, pushing the blade toward the thick end of the fillet. Try to keep from cutting through the skin or cutting too much into the flesh. On a small- to medium-size fish, such as barramundi, you should be able to keep cutting under the meat right to the end. With bigger fish, such as salmon, you may have to flop the meat over upon itself to relieve a bit of pressure on the knife. Once the knife cuts through, remove and discard the skin.

3. Remove any lingering blood or dirt with the tip of your knife. Some fish have a glossy section of fat along the bottom or stomach section of the fillet; cut away any obvious fat.

4. Repeat this process with the other fillet. You should end up with almost all the meat in two even sections.

5. Rinse the skinned fillets quickly under cool running water and pat dry.

Don't be discouraged if you are unable to cleanly fillet or skin the fish with ease the first few times you do it. With practice, you will develop a "feel" for it and be able to gauge the angle and pressure needed to make the different cuts. Although it's very useful to use a thin knife to clean and fillet a fish, it's more important to use a *sharp* knife.

Fishing and Farming Methods

BOTTOM CULTURE

Used in shellfish farming, mostly for oysters and clams. Shellfish can be broadcast on a leased area (you can't buy water, as you can land, but you can lease it from the federal government) or placed in mesh bags. Bottom culture can be helpful in slowing down growth, to thicken shells, and to eliminate the need for sinking the fish in the fall to avoid ice. Some of the downsides are potential for silt/sand to get into the fish, and easier access for predators (for example, crabs, starfish, and sponges).

CLOSED-CONTAINMENT AQUACULTURE

Land-based facilities, which may or may not be next to the water. Closed-containment aquaculture can be used for finfish or shellfish. Water is typically recirculated throughout the facility. Beneficial bacteria and filters are used to keep the water clean, and various methods are employed to re-oxygenate the water. An expensive method of farming, but one that is harmless to the ocean and wild fish stocks.

DIVER-CAUGHT

Just as it sounds, someone dons scuba gear and goes below to hand-pick shellfish, usually scallops or sea urchins. Many menus will list "diver-caught" scallops. The reality is that less than 1 percent of scallops are truly diver-caught. A true diver-caught scallop is very rare.

DREDGING

Similar to bottom trawling, in that fishing gear is dragged behind the boat. The net is much smaller, though, and so the amount of bottom that is disturbed is much less. Dredging is typically used to harvest shellfish, such as scallops, oysters, and clams. Bycatch tends to be low, with large mesh and turtle deflectors employed to help with this problem. As well, fishing areas are closely monitored, and are "closed" on a rotating basis to ensure that ocean floors can recover.

GILL NET

Also known as "drift net," this method involves hanging a net between a boat and the shore or between two boats. The amount of flotation can be modified, as well as mesh size. Gill nets allow for selective fishing, in that non-targeted sizes of fish are allowed to escape. The targeted fish become tangled in the net or their head gets in but bodies won't, so they get trapped by their gills as they try to back out. This method can be used for a wide variety of fish, both inshore and deep water. Gill nets can stretch for up to 3.2 kilometres (2 miles), and can be problematic for porpoises, whales, and turtles.

HAND-DUG

Typically only used for certain types of clams and other mollusks. Hand-digging is done close to shore, and at particular times only — when the tide is completely out or just about. It involves crawling in shallow water in a wetsuit and using a clam hack, or standing on the flats with a hack or rake. Hand-digging is very labour-intensive and seasonal. There are zero bycatch problems or environmental concerns, except if fishing in closed areas, which may be high in bacteria or toxins.

HANDLINE

One of the oldest and most effective methods of fishing. Handline fishing involves one or more baited hooks on a line that is cast from shore or a boat. The fisher can use either the "troll and pole" or "jigging" methods (see below), depending on the species of fish they are trying to catch. Handlining is used in both freshwater and ocean environments, and for many species. There is very low bycatch or environmental damage, but handlining is obviously a less-efficient harvest method.

TROLL AND POLE

Handlines are hung from a boat and pulled through the water. Effective for species such as tuna.

JIG

Handlines are pulled in quick movements, enticing targeted fish to bite. Very common for fish such as squid.

HARPOON

Just as you might imagine it: The fisher (or a spotter) visually identifies the fish, gets close to it, launches the harpoon (usually attached to a rope), and pulls in the fish.

Obviously, harpooning is used for larger fish, such as swordfish and tuna. This method has zero bycatch and no negative environmental consequences. It's very labour intensive, but fish can often be sold at a premium to compensate.

HOOK AND LINE
Typically refers to handlining (see page 288).

LONGLINE
Lines ranging from hundreds of metres to 50 kilometres (31 miles) are pulled behind a boat. The lines can have thousands of baited hooks and be set at different depths. Longlining can be used for a wide variety of species, most typically in ocean environments. The potential for bycatch is large, and much of the bycatch ends up dead, especially on particularly long lines as it takes a while to haul them in. Bycatch is monitored, though, and fishers in certain areas are expected to have quotas for several species so that throwback is minimized. Seabirds and turtles can get hooked, inadvertently, so crews must be trained to be able to release them quickly when they're pulled aboard.

OFF-BOTTOM CULTURE
Used in shellfish aquaculture. Off-bottom culture uses a floating line, and sometimes mesh bags that keep the shellfish suspended from the bottom. This method reduces predators, extends growing seasons, and makes for easier harvesting. This sort of aquaculture takes place on a leased area of water.

OPEN-CAGE/NET-PEN
This is what most people think of when they hear the words "fish farming." Open-cage farming employs nets that are open at the top but enclosed on the sides and bottom, usually in groups of eight to twelve in a bay. Though the terms are used interchangeably, there is a big difference between the two methods: "Net-pen" refers to an enclosed net that touches the sea bottom, whereas an "open-cage" is totally enclosed underneath. Both styles have been the subject of controversy over the years for various reasons, including fish waste, escaping fish, unsightly farms, and disease/parasites. Evolving practices have eliminated many of these concerns, but one main advantage of cage over pen is that cages can be moved to deep-water areas where these potential problems can be addressed even more thoroughly.

POT

Pot (or trap) fishing is primarily used in the lobster and crab fisheries, although pots are being used for some finfish species as well. Whatever the fishery or pot design, the concept is generally the same: A small netted structure is attached to a long line and submerged, usually with bait, to attract the desired species. Pots are then pulled up at regular intervals (usually once a day, but sometimes more frequently) to check for fish. They are emptied, with any bycatch thrown back, re-baited, and submerged again. This method is very gentle on the environment and on bycatch, as the fish is generally pulled up alive and unharmed.

SEINE

A similar method to gill-netting, in that a hanging net is employed, but the fish are trapped by enclosing the net rather than getting trapped in the net itself. There are generally three different forms of seine: haul, drum, and purse. Haul is not very common these days, as it was typically used in rivers and requires a lot of manpower. Drum and purse are open-ocean methods, and require powerful motors to haul in the nets. Purse-seining is the most common form. The net is circled around a school of fish, and the bottom is closed by pulling a purse string, or line, to keep the fish from escaping downward. For certain tightly schooling fish, like mackerel and sardines, this is a very efficient fishing method that minimizes bycatch and impact on the environment. For other species, such as tuna, this method tends to bring in many unwanted fish, including dolphins. As well, fish aggregating devices (FAD), which are placed in the water before the net is closed, will attract many unwanted species. Thus, seining is under scrutiny for all but schooling fish.

TONGING

Used primarily for the harvest of oysters, clams, and mussels, tonging involves the use of a single- or double-handled rake to dig for shellfish. The rake or tong is then pulled up and the contents are sorted. Any unwanted creatures are thrown back, usually with no harm done. Tonging can disturb the ocean bottom slightly, but it is considered quite gentle overall, and the bycatch is zero. A very labour-intensive method but very good for the health of the fishery.

TRAP OR TRAP NET
See *Pot*, above.

TRAWL

Common but controversial fishing method involving the dragging of a conical net behind either one or two boats. The trawl nets can be designed to fish right on the seabed (bottom trawl) or just above it (midwater trawl). Bottom trawling typically captures a significant amount of unwanted bycatch, much of which is killed by the fishing method and is discarded. Efforts are increasing to add bycatch-reducing equipment to the gear, but it is not foolproof and enforcement is inconsistent. In addition, the technique is very destructive to the ocean floor. The net has a set of wheels and a method for keeping the mouth open. It stirs up the bottom and makes noise, which attracts fish. It is considered by some to be the most destructive form of fishing, and has been outlawed in many fishing jurisdictions. Midwater trawling tends to be more selective in its catch, but still is not without problems. As well, much trawling is done in international waters, where there is very little control.

TROLLING

See *Handline*, page 288.

WEIR FISHING

One of the oldest methods of catching fish, weirs are structures built into the sea floor, such as posts, that have netting strung between them. The whole structure is shaped so that fish get funnelled toward a couple of holding areas that typically get checked by the fisher once or twice daily. The fish are mostly pushed into the first channel by water flow — and would eventually find their way out — but get trapped long enough for the fisher to take advantage. This method is still employed worldwide, though less and less in developed countries. Up to a few years ago, weirs were considered to have a minimal impact on global fish capture, as they were thought to be used on a very small scale, but a 2013 study showed that weir use is seriously underreported and might actually be having a greater impact than first thought. It is not a particularly selective capture method and tends to have a high percentage of juvenile fish, along with some bycatch. It can, however, be valuable in controlling the spread of invasive species due to its efficiency at blocking an entire river or waterway.

GLOSSARY

AQUACULTURE Also referred to as "farmed" or "cultivated." In the seafood world, these terms are more or less interchangeable, but the methods are wildly different. Some fish are raised in small bays or flooded areas, while others are grown on land in containment or closed systems, and yet others are grown in the open ocean in pens or cages. Some fish are fed, some are given antibiotics, while others subsist on food that occurs naturally in the water. The method of farming is potentially more important to the health and/or quality of the fish than whether it is farmed or wild.

BACTERIA See *Toxins and bacteria*.

BIOMASS Amount of living material in a defined amount of water. Usually helps to determine whether there may be too much fish/shellfish in a bay or to determine the overall health of a stock.

BLOODLINE A long section of flesh in a fish that is darker and typically has a stronger flavour than the surrounding flesh. Often removed.

BRINE CURING A preservation method in which the flesh of a fish is fully immersed in water that has been mixed with curing agents (such as salt, along with sugar, herbs, and spices, if desired). Takes effect more quickly than dry curing, and is better for thicker cuts and medium to larger whole fish. See also *Dry curing*.

BYCATCH Unexpected or unwanted fish that is harvested alongside targeted fish. Methods of dealing with bycatch vary with the fishery. Some bycatch is kept, usually up to a limit, while some fisheries require all bycatch to be discarded. Most fisheries try to eliminate bycatch completely via methods or specialized gear.

CEVICHE A Peruvian fish preparation in which cold raw fish is marinated in acid (for example, lime juice) for a period of time, which denatures the proteins in the fish, causing it to become opaque and producing a firm texture that mimics "cooking." See also *Crudo*.

CRUDO An Italian fish preparation in which cold raw fish is sliced thinly and then lightly dressed with olive oil and an acid (for example, lemon juice). See also *Ceviche*.

CULTIVATED See *Aquaculture*.

DASHI A type of stock, Japanese in origin. Traditionally made by boiling seaweed and cured bonito in water, and then straining the resulting liquid. Now most commonly obtained in powder or pre-made liquid form. Adds umami, or depth of flavour, to dishes.

DORY A small boat used for fishing various in-shore products. Typically flat-bottomed to allow work in shallower water.

DRY CURING A preservation method in which salt or other curing agents are infused into flesh, removing moisture and extending shelf life. Typically used on thinner cuts and smaller fish. See also *Brine curing*.

FISH AGGREGATING DEVICE (FAD) A floating structure, similar to a large buoy, that emits a certain tone or rhythm that attracts fish. Very controversial, as these attract many varieties of fish, not just targeted fish, which leads to higher bycatch rates. Avoid purchasing fish caught in this manner, if possible.

FARMED FISH See *Aquaculture*.

FISH FARM A designated body of water that can be used exclusively by one fisher or farmer. Water is not for sale and can only be leased from the government. Also referred to as a "lease."

FILLET, STEAK, LOIN Fillets and loins are typically boneless, though not always skinless. Loins are typically thicker cuts from larger fish. Steaks are cut across the backbone, contain varying levels of bone, and are always skin-on. While steaks are more cost effective for a fish shop, they have fallen out of fashion due to the public's aversion to bones.

GRAPESEED OIL Pressed from the seeds of grapes. A cooking oil with a high smoke point, which means that it remains stable when exposed to high heat. Good for searing. Avocado oil and peanut oil are good substitutes.

GRILLING Cooking over an open flame or hot coals on a grate.

HARVEST Can be used either in the wild or on the farm. Both indicate quantity obtained, as opposed to just a bounty at the end of a growing season.

LEASE See *Fish farm.*

LIQUOR Usually used to describe the juice produced by shellfish when meat is removed raw. Most liquor is clear, with some exceptions. Blood clams, for example, produce a red liquor.

POACH/POACHING To cook food by fully immersing it in liquid over low heat.

PORTION/PORTION SIZE In this book, portions are considered to be 150 to 175 g (5 to 6 oz) of meat.

SEARING Cooking on a solid piece of metal over high heat.

SIPHON In clams, the siphon is the part of the clam that will project up from beneath the sand. It allows for the flow of water into and out of the clam. It also gives away the clam's location, and can be retracted quickly in an attempt at self-preservation.

SMOKING (HOT AND COLD) Smoking is a secondary technique for preserving fish, after curing. "Hot smoking" is done at a high temperature for a short period of time, and produces a "cooked" product. Hot smoked products have a shorter shelf life than cold smoked products. "Cold smoking" is done at a much lower temperature over a longer period of time; the fish texture remains more raw, but the flesh is typically lower in water content and will keep longer after smoking.

SUSTAINABLE/RESPONSIBLE/THOUGHTFUL Terms that have no clear definition yet have become popular when talking about fishing and fish farming. "Sustainable" is most common. Typically refers to a well-managed wild fishery that is fished at a level that supports the proliferation of the overall biomass. Farmed fish is by default sustainable, though some certification organizations frown upon it. "Responsible" and "thoughtful" can be used to indicate that fish workers are also treated well and environmental practices are considered. In general, these are all new considerations in the seafood world, and as such are not equally applied across all fisheries.

SWEAT To cook vegetables such as onions and garlic in a small amount of oil, over low heat, to allow softening and caramelization to occur.

TOXINS AND BACTERIA Potential hazards in food. Bacteria (for example, *Salmonella* and *E. coli*) can be minimized via washing and/or heat. Toxins, however, will linger even after washing and cooking. Toxins such as *Clostridium botulinum* (botulism) and domoic acid (which causes amnesic shellfish poisoning) are much more dangerous than bacteria, as they generally can't be eliminated once the food reaches the consumer.

YIELD When talking about fish and shellfish, yield refers to the amount of usable meat that can be extracted from the creature — that is, the size of the mussel meat in the shell or the ratio of meat to bones and viscera after filleting a fish

Acknowledgements

Thank you!

To Rick O'Brien, for your hard work and beautiful photography.

To the industry: The entire Honest Weight staff (past and present), Victoria Bazan, Marc Beaudin, Phyllis and Robert Carr, Max Daigle, Derek Dammann, Sean Dimin, George Dowdle, Hugue Dufour, Johnny and Leo Flynn, Rob Hyndman, Charlotte Langley, Matty Matheson, the team at Maximum Seafood, Martin O'Brien, Sarah Obraitis, Michael and Anna Olson, Martin Picard, Chris Pipergias, and the entire crew at Rodney's Oyster House.

To the backbones: Mary and Howard McKeown; Dave and Alina Flaherty, Leslie Flaherty, Mark Flaherty, Cassandra Loomans, and Anna Flaherty; Rob and Lyn Bethune; Lo Bil; Chris Campbell; Joanne and Mark Campbell; Evan Cranley; Allison, Henry, Ivan, and Eleanor Cunningham-Morin; Jillian Dickens; Dave Dundas; Christine Fancy; Vanya Filipovic; Marc-Olivier Frappier; Sue Gingras; Norm, Lucas, and Theo Hardie; Chris Johns; Tommy Kelly; Sean Kozey; Laleh Larijani; Dylan Ledoux; Andrea Mastandrea; Mark McKeown; Amy Millan; David MacMillan; Chris Nuttall-Smith; Isabelle Patenaude; the Pendergast Clan; and Devon Thom.

A very special thank you to Dr. Christina Lee and John Delos-Reyes; Dr. Teresa Petrella; Dr. Marcus Butler; and Dr. Paolo Mazzotta.

And to John Petcoff, Frédéric Morin, and Maude-Isabelle Delagrave; and Sarah MacLachlan, Douglas Richmond, Alex Trnka, Laura Brady, Maria Golikova, Greg Tabor, Tracy Bordian, Sarah Howden, Ruth Pincoe, and the entire team at House of Anansi, who all believed so strongly in this book, and had the courage and determination to see it through to the end.

Recipe Index

INDEX

JOHN BIL (1968–2018) worked with fish — on the water, behind the counter, and in the kitchen — for over twenty-five years. Bil began his career shucking oysters at the Toronto dining institution Rodney's Oyster House before venturing east to the Maritimes, where he spent over a decade working in the shellfish and fish farming industry and later opened his first restaurant, Ship to Shore, in Darnley, P.E.I. A respected and in-demand seafood expert, Bil assisted with the openings of several other high-profile restaurants, including M. Wells Steakhouse (New York), Claddagh Oyster House (Charlottetown, P.E.I.), Restaurant Joe Beef (Montreal), and most recently, his own Honest Weight (Toronto).

RICK O'BRIEN is a lifestyle and food photographer with over twenty years' experience working with Michelin-star chefs, musicians, architects, interior designers, and international hotel and travel companies. Originally from St. John's, Newfoundland, Rick lives with his partner and two dogs in Toronto.